Mike V.

RAY

Ted E Bear K.

Mike Carolon

Scott Bird

Larry Tarallo

R Wadell
"WAZ"

Rick Abernathy

WARRIORS
AND
SPECIAL OLYMPICS

THE WERTZ WARRIORS STORY

RICHARD L. BALDWIN

Buttonwood Press, LLC
Haslett, MI

WARRIORS AND SPECIAL OLYMPICS:
THE WERTZ WARRIORS STORY

by Richard L. Baldwin

Copyright © 2006 Buttonwood Press

Manufactured in the United States of America.

First Edition.
ISBN 0-9742920-4-4

Published by Buttonwood Press
P.O. Box 716
Haslett, Michigan 48840

www.buttonwoodpress.com

DISCLAIMER:

*Every effort was made to assure accuracy in this book. The data was received from the Wertz Warrior of-
fice. Drafts were reviewed by Wertz Warriors who were asked to do so by the Board President. In the event
that a name is misspelled, a story is inaccurate, or a date is in error, please accept the apology of the author and publisher, who bears full responsibility for the content of this book. Perhaps in advance of this
book's sale and distribution I can borrow a famous quote, "To err is human, to forgive, divine."*

A PERSONAL NOTE TO THE WARRIORS:

It was a pleasure to write this book for you.
Thanks for inviting me on the 2003 ride and making me
feel welcome. I have the same deep respect and admiration
for you that all of your fans and admirers have, and my
thoughts echo all the praise that comes to you through
these pages of quotes and memories.

I will wear my Green Jacket with great pride and
thankfulness for you as an organization and as individuals.
You've given me a wonderful lesson in selfless giving.

I hope you enjoy your story.
— *Rich Baldwin, Author*

ODE TO A WERTZ WARRIOR

None of you will be shocked to find,
When you're ranked among your peers,
There's a special place in heaven,
For Wertz Warrior Volunteers!
There won't be membership meetings,
or forms you must complete,
No raffles rule, investment pools
and no accounting receipts!
There won't be Tracy babbling on,
or machines that never break,
No bumps, no bruises,
no muscles that ache,
no thawed rivers, ponds or lakes.
No luggage to move from place to place,
And snow conditions made to race,
Temperatures that'll be just right,
There's a fridge filled with cold Bud Light.
Your good deeds will be recognized,
You'll receive undying thanks!
The money will flow, for Special O
Insuring your historic ranks.
And as you settle in up there,
You'll realize your true worth,
'Cause you'll be served
with smiles and heart,
Just like you served on Earth!

THANK YOU, WERTZ WARRIORS!
Written by Neil Foster

This book is dedicated to the athletes who participate in the Special Olympics Michigan Programs.

These athletes provide the opportunity for the Wertz Warriors and the thousands of people who support them to donate time, energy, and well-earned money to open their hearts to service.

ACKNOWLEDGEMENTS

There are so many people who have worked hard to see that this story is told. In no particular order, I wish to thank Vic Battani, president of the Wertz Warriors Board for his support. The Buttonwood Press team is to be thanked for a lot of intense work: thank you Alisa Miller, editor; Joyce Wagner, proofreader; Sarah Thomas, cover designer and typesetter. I wish to thank the Wertz Warriors and all the men who submitted information for this book. I wish to thank Bob Sassanella and Dave White for assisting in photo selection. I wish to thank *The Detroit News* for permission to reprint a series of articles by the late Joe Falls. Finally, I thank Tim Kavanagh for coordinating this project on behalf of the Warriors.

— *Rich Baldwin*
Author and Publisher

"I would like to take this opportunity to thank the current and past boards of directors, the riders, support crew, and the thousands and thousands of people who have donated their time, energy and money over the 25 years that we have raised money for Special Olympics Michigan. Without people like you, Wertz Warriors would not have been able to achieve the over six million dollars we have raised since 1982.

"I would also like to thank Rich Baldwin for donating his time and energy in writing this book and Dennis Kavanagh, the president and owner of Data Reproductions for donating the cost of printing this book. Finally, thanks to Tim Kavanagh for his work with Rich in advising and researching material for this book.

"God Bless all of you."

— *Victor R. Battani*
Chairman, Wertz Warriors Board of Directors

"I would like to take this opportunity to thank the Wertz Warriors for all of their hard work. The athletes of Special Olympics Michigan cherish you as you ride for them. Without the dedication of the Warriors, Special Olympics Michigan's Winter Games wouldn't be as spectacular. Thanks, too, to Rich Baldwin who rode with the Warriors in 2003 and wrote this book. You are all special and the athletes of Special Olympics Michigan thank you."

— *Kam Waryas*
President, Special Olympics Michigan Board of Directors

INTRODUCTION

The Wertz Warriors received their name from the famous Detroit Sports journalist, Joe Falls, who accompanied the Warriors on two of their rides in 1983 and 1991. He described the men as a collection of heroes who have a passion for speed over snow but more importantly, have a passion for service, and for giving back to people less fortunate then they.

More specifically, the group is an example of one man's dream transformed into reality. Vic Wertz, a former Detroit Tigers All-Star, had a dream to underwrite the cost of the annual Michigan Special Olympics Winter Games. Following his baseball career, Vic owned a Miller Beer Distributorship in Mt. Clemens. In 1981 he set out to enlist many of his friends to help him with his dream. A small group of men considered a variety of ways to generate the money needed to fund the Winter Games. One of the initial suggestions involved rolling beer barrels from Mt. Clemens to Milwaukee, the home of Miller Brewing Company. Realizing that the reality of distance and weather would be too much to overcome, they decided that they would become involved in endurance snowmobiling. So, the idea was born, and the Wertz Warriors became a reality. The Wertz Warriors have grown from a modest size of 31 riders and 15 support crew in 1982 to an expected 90 riders and support crew on the 2006 anniversary ride. Over the past 25 years, approximately 320 Warriors have participated in the 25 rides.

These Warriors come from all walks of life. There are many jobs to perform supporting the riders — fuel trucks, mechanics with tools and spare parts, medical personnel, semi-truck drivers to haul the machines, a snowmobile headquarters, memorabilia sales personnel, and countless numbers of vendors who donate time, money and supplies to make the ride a reality. These volunteers join hands with the endurance snowmobilers to put smiles on the faces of the Special Olympics athletes.

This book will provide information, stories, and memories, and will serve as a tribute to all the Warriors who over the past 25 years have successfully raised $6,495,000.00 for Special Olympics Michigan while riding 122,112 collective miles or 16,602 miles per machine. An additional $773,398.80 has been raised and has been put into a restricted fund.

YEAR	NUMBER OF RIDERS	NUMBER OF SUPPORT	MILES PER MACHINE	COLLECTIVE MILES	WINTER GAMES FUNDING
1982	31	—	436	13,516	$35,000.00
1983	45	—	525	23,625	$65,000.00
1984	37	23	730	27,010	$80,000.00
1985	45	19	927	41,715	$135,000.00
1986	45	20	792	35,640	$200,000.00
1987	44	21	657	28,908	$235,000.00
1988	50	25	692	34,600	$250,000.00
1989	47	28	613	28,811	$265,000.00
1990	49	30	550	26,950	$265,000.00
1991	48	27	210	10,080	$270,000.00
1992	47	27	640	30,080	$280,000.00
1993	48	27	650	31,200	$280,000.00
1994	54	28	813	43,902	$280,000.00
1995	56	27	845	47,320	$280,000.00
1996	56	30	870	48,720	$300,000.00
1997	62	28	865	53,630	$328,000.00
1998	62	29	335	20,770	$343,000.00
1999	71	27	720	51,120	$350,000.00
2000	68	30	866	58,888	$385,000.00
2001	67	30	855	57,285	$347,000.00
2002	69	32	270	18,630	$372,000.00
2003	71	32	870	62,640	$405,000.00
2004	72	32	1031	74,232	$390,000.00
2005	57	33	840	47,880	$355,000.00
GRAND TOTALS:			16,602	122,112	$6,495,000.00

PREFACE

"When I first began in my new job as Executive Director in 1990, I knew I would be working more directly with the Wertz Warriors. This was something I looked forward to, but was intimidated by. I knew this to be a big, burly group of snowmobiling men but I didn't know much else about them.

"At the first meeting, I worked my way around the room and tried to meet most of the men who were all part of this tremendous snowmobile endurance ride. I finally settled at one table with some of the leaders of the organization and began getting to know them better. That was a night I will never forget.

"The first thing I noticed was their size. This was a big group. There were at least 50 riders and a support crew of 25 who participated in this ride. We were all packed into a meeting room of one of the rider's establishments and it was crowded. Not only were there a lot of them, but they were big! These are guys that lift snowmobiles with one arm, ride hundreds of miles in freezing conditions, and live on the edge! Or at least that is what I thought.

"The second thing I noticed was the bond they held and the affection they had for each other. They are jokesters and like to have a good time. Yes, they were there to be a part of this prestigious fund-raising group; yes, they were serious snow-loving snowmobilers, but they really enjoyed each other's company and made it really fun to be around.

"Some had been with Vic Wertz when he created the idea of the ride and had ridden with him the first time. Their fierce loyalty to him and his vision was clearly obvious. They spoke fondly of Vic and were committed to making his dream of sponsoring the Special Olympics State Winter Games a reality. It didn't matter where any of the riders came from, where they worked, or in what position. They were united on this front.

"However, what struck me most was why they were doing the ride. They were really committed to the athletes of Special Olympics. They were and still are today, there to raise money for Special Olympics athletes, so that they can experience winter sports. The Wertz Warriors know the money they raise goes toward a great cause and can see the impact on the faces of the athletes.

"The highlight for the riders is to see the athletes at the State Winter Games and to give them rides on their snowmobiles. The athletes really love the Wertz Warriors and look forward to seeing them at the games. Lasting friendships have been born here and continue for years and years. The Wertz Warriors individually really are generous people and have enormous hearts. They are fortunate to have the support of loving and caring families that allow them to do this tremendous ride.

"It has been my pleasure to know these men and their families. I salute the Wertz Warriors and their efforts."

— Lois Arnold
President and CEO of Special Olympics Michigan

ABOUT SPECIAL OLYMPICS MICHIGAN

The mission of our organization is to provide sports training and athletic competition in a variety of Olympic-type sports for the children and adults with intellectual disabilities who live in our state. Athletes are given continuing opportunities to develop physical fitness; to demonstrate courage; to experience joy; and to participate in a sharing of gifts, skills, and friendship with their families, other Special Olympics athletes, and the community.

The athletes are young and old. They have different backgrounds and hometowns. Some are gifted athletes; others must work very hard just to reach the finish line.

Over 14,000 athletes participate in Special Olympics Michigan programs. Michigan has one of the largest programs in the U.S., but we're always looking for more athletes! Although sports are the "vehicle," the ultimate goal of Special Olympics is to help persons with intellectual disabilities participate and receive respect as members of their communities. Through Special Olympics, athletes gain self-confidence and prove their own capabilities. Special Olympics Michigan is not just training for sports — it's training for life!

TO OBTAIN FURTHER INFORMATION:

Special Olympics Michigan
Central Michigan University
Mount Pleasant, MI USA 48859

(800) 644-6404 or (989) 774-3911
Fax (989) 774-3034

Web site: somi@somi.org

FOREWORD

"My first contact with the Wertz Warriors came eleven years ago at Sugar Loaf Mountain in northern Michigan. While I really did not know what to make of the group of 'gentle giants' at the time, I have since learned a great deal. They are a group of people from all walks of life who spend all year raising money for Special Olympics Michigan and the privilege of spending a week of their vacation time (some only get one week per year) to ride over 900 miles on snowmobiles throughout Michigan. I have also learned that the most important part of the ride for every Warrior is arriving at Winter Games to give rides to athletes and attending opening ceremonies. Nothing touches me more than to see the interactions between these Warriors and our Special Olympians. We all owe a great debt of gratitude to the Wertz Warriors for their continued commitment to Special Olympics Michigan. THANK YOU WARRIORS!

— *Robert E. Chadwick II*

Former President, Special Olympics Michigan Board of Directors

WARRIORS
AND
SPECIAL OLYMPICS
THE WERTZ WARRIORS STORY

CHAPTER 1

How it All Began

Vic Wertz is known to most baseball fans and scholars of the game as an All-Star baseball player for the Detroit Tigers and the Cleveland Indians. He was a power-hitter who earned spots on the American League All-Star roster in 1949, 1951, 1952, and 1957. He was voted Most Valuable Player in 1949, 1959, 1956, 1957, and 1960.

Vic Wertz was the hitter, who in game one of the 1954 World Series, hit the long fly ball to deep center field that gave Willie Mays the opportunity to make the historic and exciting over-the-shoulder catch that became one of his trademarks. In his 17 seasons, Wertz played in 1,862 games and got 1,692 hits, including 266 home runs. On September 14, 1947 at Washington, Vic Wertz hit for the cycle (a single, a double, a triple and a home run all in a single game) and became the first Tiger to do so in the post-World War II era. George Kell and Hoot Evers did it in 1950. After that it wasn't until 1993 that Travis Fryman accomplished the feat. Hitting for the cycle is a rare accomplishment and Vic Wertz holds that distinction.

Yet there was another side to Vic Wertz, a side that the baseball fan could not see, one which his friend and business associates were well aware of. According to Bill McInnis, Donald "Digger" O'Dell, and Fred Duemling, first and foremost Vic Wertz was a compassionate man. In addition, he was very concerned with image and cleanliness. He expected and demanded that his warehouse be immaculate. At the end-of-the-ride party, as a sign of respect, Vic required the Warriors to wear a suit and tie. People did not argue with Vic Wertz. You followed his orders and if there was any type of disagreement, he would invite you to lunch and forget about the altercation.

Bill described Vic as, "The greatest guy you'd ever want to meet. You couldn't say a bad word about him." Digger added that, "He always had a smile on his face. He was a nice guy with a commanding presence. He had a good handle on remembering names." Bill recalled that when Vic would be having a meal in a restaurant or a bar, he would always pick up the tab and demand that he do so.

Warrior Carl Hart of Lewiston, says of Vic Wertz, "He was one of the nicest guys I ever met in my life!" Pete Petoskey, also of Lewiston, adds, "Vic Wertz was a favorite Tiger to me along with Hal Newhouser, Charlie Gehringer, Hank Greenberg, Mickey Cochrane, Gates Brown and others who represented several different eras in my memory of Tigers history. Vic Wertz, when starting the Warriors, included many men and women that have helped through the years. In that group was a special friend, Tom May of Lewiston. The Special Olympics, with my grandson having been a participant, are doing a world of good in building, confidence, competitiveness, and strength in our children."

Vic Wertz and his associates wanted to raise money to help children with disabilities. Perhaps the reason for choosing this particular group of people to support originated from the fact that in 1955, in the midst of his career, Vic Wertz contracted a non-paralyzing form of polio. He recovered, rejoined the Cleveland Indians, and went on with his legendary baseball career. This was part of his motivation to give back and to serve children in need. According to Digger O'Dell, "Vic had a passion to help those less fortunate than himself." He already sponsored a successful summer golf outing, but was looking for a winter fund-raiser.

Over lunch one day, Vic Wertz, Mitch Cohoon, Roger Pype, and Bill McInnis came up with the idea to have an endurance snowmobile ride. Bill, who (according to Fred Duemling) was Wertz's "right-hand man," was responsible for running everything outside the office; the warehouse, the semi-drivers, the mechanics. Bill is also the last active Warrior of the original committee of men who went back to the office and proposed the idea to Fred Duemling and Ed Palenkas, Sr., and in essence, created the Wertz Warriors. They found favor with the idea and talked with businessmen Larry King and Roy Heisner, and by the end of the day and a lot of talk, they had a plan.

The initial ride was by necessity something of an experiment, but its success paved the way for a great tradition of fund-raising and memories. The first riders, 31 in number, along with 15 support people, rode their snowmobiles and support vehicles out of the parking lot of Vic's Miller Beer Distributorship in January of 1982. Their goal was to ride to Mackinaw City and they made it. Vic paid all of the expenses associated with the trip so that all donations made to the ride would go to partially pay for the Special Olympics Winter Games. The goal was to raise $20,000 but they exceeded their goal and gave Special Olympics Michigan a check for $35,000.00. It was Vic's goal to pay the full price for the Winter Games within five years. That goal was reached in advance of five years. By the fourth year, the Warriors had raised sufficient funds to pay for the entire Winter Games.

As Vic was a distributor for Miller beer, there was plenty of beer for everyone associated with the ride. Cases of beer were transported in the back of the gasoline truck. Bill McInnis recalls that, "Every time you stopped you could come to the truck and get gas or beer. We stopped a lot!" In those first couple of years, fifty cases of beer were frozen each year being transported in the gasoline truck.

Fred Duemling recalls that an ambulance accompanied the first group, as did an undersheriff from Macomb County. He recalls that it was a well-planned trip, but often they did not reach their destination and would need to do some night driving.

A sheriff would often provide escorts. In the early days, there was not the network of snowmobile trails that exists today, but there was a lot of snow, so movement along county roads was easier. There were lunches at local chambers of commerce. The Knights of Columbus were supportive in the first year, the Lions were supportive in the second year, and in the third year, the Northern Michigan Moose Association began their support which continues to this day.

Digger O'Dell remembers that in year two a single-engine support plane was along to provide a view from the sky. A couple of air-to-ground radios were used to report any accidents or breakdowns along the route. Members of the support crew took turns in the plane to act as spotters.

Following Vic's untimely death in 1983, according to Digger O'Dell and Bill McInnis, "It was Kenny Hintz, who was a super, pat-on-the-back type guy, who held us together. We needed one person to keep this going, and Kenny was the right man for the time. Kenny was warmly welcomed by those who knew him whenever he appeared." Carl Hart also approached the famous Tigers catcher Bill Freeham and asked him to help fill the void in leadership. He became the honorary chairman, and rode from 1984 to 1989. Mickey Lolich, Jack Morris, and Mickey Stanley offered support by going on a ride or making an appearance or two. Mark "The Bird" Fidrych is the current honorary ride chairman. Mark has ridden and served in this honorary role every year since 1994.

Long time rider Tony Pype reflects, "I think of the old days in 1982 when I was first asked by my uncle, Roger Pype, to go on the 1983 ride. I felt very privileged and honored. I knew of Vic Wertz and his baseball career. My uncle had invited me to some of the other functions that Vic had been involved in. I thought that this was going to be a great opportunity to participate with a sport celebrity and have a great time snowmobiling and partying out on the road. I was right, it was a great time. But, I learned so much about life that year. I learned that Vic Wertz was more than a celebrity; he was a special man with a very huge heart. He was an inspiration to all he came in contact with. When he walked into a room, the room seemed to light up. He was kind and soft-spoken, but he got his point across with class. He wanted to help Special Olympics with the snowmobile ride. Vic would be there for anybody, or any cause, anytime. He was a genuine great man and it was an honor to have known him."

"Whereas once he was known as a former major-leaguer who started doing something nice for special kids, Wertz today is probably better remembered as someone who did something nice for special kids ... who also happened to play major-league baseball."

— George Pohly
The Macomb Daily, 1994
(used with permission)

Ken Maly speaks for all the Warriors when he says, 'Thank God for Vic Wertz — one person can make a difference!"

The following is taken from BaseballHistorian.com in their section titled, American Heroes:

Vic Wertz — Outfielder and 1B, Bats Left Throws Right, Detroit Tigers 1947-1952 and 1962-1963; St. Louis Browns 1953-54, Cleveland 1954-1958; Boston Red Sox 1959-1961.

Power-packed, clutch hitter, Vic Wertz starred for the Detroit Tigers with his torrid hitting in the late 1940s. In 1947, Vic Wertz blasted 26 doubles, 20 HR's, batted .304 and knocked in 133 runs. In 1950, his stats were 37 D, 27 HR's, batted .308 with 123 RBI's. Traded to the St. Louis Browns in 1953, Vic hit 19 HR's. While with Cleveland in late 1954, he was a major force for the Indians winning the pennant. In 1956 with the Indians, Wertz hit 32 HR's and had 106 RBI's and the following year hit 28 HR's with 105 RBI's. Vic Wertz was a popular slugger wherever he grabbed a bat, drawing loud cheers from his many fans. Wertz always found time to honor requests for autographed photos."

CHAPTER 2

The Great Snowfari

Joe Falls, legendary sports writer for The Detroit News, went along on two trips with the Wertz Warriors. His first was the second year (in 1983), and at that time he wrote daily articles which were sent back to the paper for printing. The seven articles were made into a small booklet titled "A Week with the Wertz Warriors." His second trip with the Warriors was in 1991. The 1983 articles are printed here with the permission of Joe Falls and The Detroit News. The 1991 articles are later in the book.

Tuesday, February 8, 1983

WERTZ WARRIORS RUN FOR TEARS AND MACKINAW CITY

PART I: THE GREAT SNOWFARI

BAY CITY — Who are these magnificent men on their flying machines ... roaring through the woods, across the frozen lakes, deep into valleys and back up the snow-covered hills of Michigan?

You might as well call them "Wertz Warriors" because that's what they sound like — 45 men roaring around the state at breakneck speeds on their snazzy snowmobiles so that handicapped children can play in the snow, too.

Crazy?

Sure, they're crazy. They went wheeling out of Vic Wertz's beer distributorship in Mt. Clemens in the soft light of Monday morning, 45 machines howling like the devil's own brigade, 45 men on a mission of love.

Lovable?

I guess you can call them that, too — 45 lovable lugs — because what they're doing they are doing for the Michigan Special Olympics, so those less fortunate than they can find some richness in their own lives.

Guess who's watching the snowmobiles — dipping and diving, twisting and turning — from the safety of a motor home, warm and snuggly, with hot coffee and Butterfinger bars at his side?

I wouldn't get out there with them for the receipts from Wertz's beer distributorship, but 44 men have joined the old Tigers slugger in this run zigzagging up and across the state so that the kids can enjoy themselves at their Winter Olympics at Sugar Loaf Mountain.

Last year, they sent 30 sleds from Mt. Clemens to Mackinaw City and raised $26,000.

This time they're aiming for $35,000, but judging from yesterday's reception in places like Berville, Attica, Lapeer and Bay City, they could easily double last year's count.

"Our eventual goal is to pay the whole bill for the Winter Games," said Wertz, who is 56 and should know better than to go tearing around the countryside on a lawnmower on skis.

Fast? They throw up the snow like rooster tails on the river, and the interesting thing is nobody makes a cent out of it — except the kids.

How do they raise the dough?

Easy.

They charge each sled $750 to take part — and they had more than 400 applications this year.

They could take only 45 because when you put that many snowmobiles out in the open, running at top speed, they stretch out for up to 3 1/2 miles and they don't want anybody getting lost in the woods. That would be hard to explain to their wives.

The truth is, they are getting tremendous support all along the route. Even before they left, the Selfridge Air National Guard Base turned over $6,000 from a spaghetti dinner and the Macomb County Sheriff's department gave them $1,600, plus an escort to the county borders. In fact, no fewer than 85 law enforcement agencies will work with them throughout the 625 mile, six-day expedition.

When they stopped at a small field in Berville for coffee and doughnuts and a refueling, the Lion's Club of Berville was on hand with a check for $1,110.

That was just for parking and saying hello.

An hour later they were in Attica, where the Sheriff's Department of Lapeer had breakfast and a $1,000 check waiting for them.

This is how it goes — it is a simple case of people helping people. Nobody talks about beer, nobody tries to sell beer. All that's in the minds of these 45 men is to reach Mackinaw City and turn over as much money as they can to the Michigan Special Olympics.

They like Mackinaw City the best — not because it is the end of the long ordeal but because that's where they pull off the road and each is given a Special Olympian to ride with them through the final few miles into town. That's when the tears do not come from the wind.

"Last year they were all bawling ... I couldn't believe it," said Kent Kukuk, one of the race officials.

It is not easy going this distance on a snowmobile. A year ago, Ed Palenkas Sr., a mere 57, complained of back pains and all but fell from his snowmobile. He suffered a kidney stone attack and was rushed to the hospital. Guess who is back on his sled for this year's snowfari?

Mitch Cohoon pulled off the road outside of Mackinaw City and complained that he couldn't see. The wind chill factor was 59 below and his eyeballs had frozen. Guess who is also back on his sled?

"Wertz Warriors" are a hardy lot.

More tomorrow from Digger O'Dell's snuggly motor home, where it's very difficult to get any sleep because of all the noise going on outside.

Wednesday, February 9, 1983

**SNOWMOBILERS $21 CLOSER TO GOAL OF $50,000:
LISTENER PASSES THE HAT IN HIGGINS LAKE TO AID
WERTZ'S SAFARI TO SPECIAL OLYMPICS**

PART II: THE GREAT SNOWFARI

GRAYLING — Wertz's Warriors — sometimes known as "The Vic Pack" rode into town last night on their howling snowmobiles, their coffers richer by $21 bucks.

That's because of the nice lady who passed the hat for them when they pulled in at the Higgins Lake Lodge for a little fuel.

It was an unscheduled pit stop, and as these 45 snowmobilers stood around filling their tanks, they began talking to each other about the kids they will see tonight at the opening ceremonies of the Winter Games of the Michigan Special Olympics at Sugar Loaf Mountain. Their words were so moving that one of the customers jumped from her seat and went around the room and collected a buck from every person in the place.

Twenty-one people, 21 bucks.

"Every little bit helps ... and she was beautiful," Vic Wertz said as he stepped off his snowmobile in the parking lot behind the Holiday Inn in Grayling last night.

Wertz, the Mt. Clemens beer baron — don't you think he looks a little like Eric Van Stroheim? — is the leader of this crazy caravan and his eyes were glowing as his guys completed the second leg of their statewide tour for the benefit of the Special Olympics.

They were going 625 miles in a six-day run and hope to collect more than $50,000.

It wasn't an easy day for them yesterday as one of their snow-mobiles broke down and two ran out of gas. The three mishaps held them up considerably and yet it was a joyous day for them — one which saw them racing madly through the woods of West Branch, Higgins Lake, Roscommon and St. Helen.

This is an odd group. They've had their share of problems but nobody has uttered a single complaint yet.

Monte Clark would never believe it — 45 guys working together in complete harmony.

This may be the purest sport of all. Nobody has an agent, nobody is going to arbitration and nobody is riding out his option.

They are all here because they want to be here. Nobody forced them into it. Each of them came up with a minimum of $750 for the privilege of driving for the handicapped kids of the state.

They are outdoorsmen and they play hard but nobody breaks up the furniture or gets nasty after dark. They are a class crew. They've got drivers in their 60s and drivers in their 20s. Age is of no consequence. The machines make them all equal. They strive as one to reach their goal.

If somebody breaks down, they all stop to help. It is really an amazing sight.

Some of these are prosperous businessmen who can write out a $750 check and think nothing of it. One of them gave $5,000.

It's not so easy for some of the others — particularly the younger drivers.

They had to resort to their wits to raise the dough to drive.

Tim Braun put on a card party and raised $250. He also bought himself a box of bottles, put some labels on them and distributed them to the bars and stores in his neighborhood, picking up the pennies, nickels, dimes and quarters once a week.

"It was crazy — I put one into a sporting goods store and the store was broken into twice. They took some guns but left the money alone both times," said Braun.

Larry Melton and Rick Drinkhorn raised $750 each by calling on private businesses. The Fountain View Bowling Lanes gave them $300. Not content, the pair ran a 1950s sock hop and raised another $1,600, which they also put into the snowmobile run.

And then there was Al Pilon, who started collecting dough but was transferred out of town.

He had gone to his barber for a donation and the barber told him all he could give him was a free haircut.

Al Pilon got the haircut — then wrote out a personal check of $12.00 for Special Olympics.

These are 'Wertz's Warriors.'

Thursday, February 10, 1983

EVERY DAY IS 'SPECIAL' FOR DIGGER

PART III: THE GREAT SNOWFARI

CEDAR, MICH. — He sits there behind the wheel with his funny little hat on his head, not unlike the way Popeye wears his own cap.

He is 46 years old and he walks like a sailor who just came in from the sea and who doesn't have his land legs yet.

You'd never know he is around because he is so quiet, but you also know he is around because he is so friendly.

His name is Digger O'Dell and he's a very special man on this Vic Wertz Snowmobile Snowfari.

He's the guy driving the motor home and, somehow, he manages to keep a lot of things together in his own quiet way.

The motor home sort of serves as a moving base for the fleet of 45 snowmobiles.

You're cold, you come in to warm up.

You're thirsty, you come in for a beer.

You're lonely — Digger will perk you up with one of his smiles.

Whenever something goes right — and a few things do — he grins and says: "Just like downtown."

He is a remarkable man. He seems at peace with himself and it is a beautiful thing to behold.

My admiration for him grows by the day.

The others are out there racing through the woods — feeling all the excitement of driving at breathtaking speeds.

When they come roaring through a town, the people stand there and gape at the magnificence of these machines.

They are stunned by the sight of 45 of them roaring by in perfect order.

The noise alone is shattering.

Digger, meanwhile, sits in the obscurity of his van, happy with his own world. Nobody knows he's around but it doesn't matter to him. He is just pleased to be a part of the scene.

You can see that the days are very special to him. He is living every one of them to the fullest.

Digger is forever on the CB, making sure everyone is all right in the support crew. They've got 10 vehicles following the snow-mobile caravan around, and they are ready to pounce into action when needed.

These machines are starting to break down from the strain of the trip. Six lost their belts yesterday. One blew a clutch.

All are rescued as quickly as possible.

Digger is always on top of things, worrying about everyone around him. He even stays in touch with the private airplane which is following the snowmobilers.

The plane points the way to the trails and helps out with lost riders.

All kinds of people are involved in this project to raise money for the Michigan Special Olympics and none is more special than Digger O'Dell. He works in the publicity department at the Selfridge Air National Guard base and it was he and Rita Rosek who got together and threw that spaghetti dinner and turned over $6,200 to Vic Wertz before the machines ever left Mt. Clemens.

Like all the rest, Digger O'Dell stood there in the darkness at the foot of Sugar Loaf Mountain last night and watched the opening ceremonies of the Winter Games of the Michigan Special Olympics.

It was a spectacular sight … with nearly 50 skiers snaking down the mountainside carrying lighted torches while the Special Olympians emblem was ignited on the side of the hill and fireworks flashed overhead.

Wherever Digger was — and I couldn't find him in the darkness — I know what he was doing.

He was watching in silence, with a small smile on his face. That's the way he has been through the whole trip.

And, he had to have an extra feeling of pride when his 45 guys came down from the mountainside with their lights blazing and chilled the 700 handicapped youngsters with their great display of driving.

Yep, if I know Digger O'Dell — and I'd like to get to know him better — he had one beautiful time for himself last night.

A far cry from those other nights when he spent 5 1/2 years in a POW camp in Vietnam.

Friday, February 11, 1983

COLD, LONG HAUL BATHED IN WARMTH: LEWISTON HAILS 'WARRIORS' AS SPECIAL OLYMPIANS SWING INTO ACTION

PART IV: THE GREAT SNOWFARI

CEDAR, MICH. — They are gone. They left in the icy darkness of the morning — 45 men on a mission of love.

You better believe it's love when they get up at 4:30 a.m. and gather by their snowmobiles at 5:30 a.m.

In these northern woods, you can't see your hand in front of your face, much less the morning sun, at 5:30 a.m. Try changing sparkplugs in a snow-blown field at 5:30 a.m.

But, these, again, are "Wertz Warriors," maybe the most dedicated group of athletes in this whole state.

They have a job to finish as they crisscross the state in their souped-up lawn mowers, earning money for the Michigan Special Olympics.

Yesterday afternoon: Lewiston.

Last night: Gaylord.

Today: Alpena.

Tomorrow: Mackinaw City … and the finish of their 625-mile, six-day adventure. On and on they go, the trails becoming more difficult with each mile.

"They're getting tired," said Kent Kukuk, a snowfari official, as the snowmobilers pulled into Gaylord last night. "Their spirits are still high but you can see the strain in some of the faces."

Some of the faces are 60 years old. Yesterday they were joined by a 70-year-old face — a guy who calls himself "The Lewiston Streaker."

He led the way into Lewiston on his own sled — clad in nothing more than his bathing suit.

It must have been a gala occasion because they let all the kids out of school and the whole town was decorated with signs, banners, streamers, bumper stickers and buttons.

All proclaiming the same thing: We care for our Special Olympians.

They were given a royal reception in Lewiston as the townsfolk collected $699 and turned it over to Vic Wertz, the head of this crazy caravan.

One of the riders — Jim Kryczak — got so excited he wrote a check for $1,000 for the Michigan Special Olympics. He had already given $750 for the right to ride for the handicapped kids, but Lewiston is his home town and he felt a little more than the others did. Call it home town pride.

It's too bad, though, they could not have stayed here at Sugar Loaf Mountain for the opening day of the Winter Games of the Michigan Special Olympics.

They would have seen another great performance — this one by Tommy Strauss from the Oakland County team.

Tommy is 28 years old. He attends the Pontiac Vocare Center, where he studies math and basic woodworking skills, such as how to use a screwdriver, hammer and nails. He lives in a group home and on this day he scaled the heights of the Matterhorn.

He won three medals in the day-long competition at the Sugar Loaf Ski Lodge:

A Gold for downhill skiing.

A Gold for speedskating.

A Silver for broomball.

"I love the Special Olympics," Tommy said, high-fiving everybody in sight as he returned to his chalet. "It's my favorite thing of all."

He was asked what he liked best about it.

"That's easy," he replied. "The dancing."

See fellers — no difference. He likes the dancing the best.

Tommy, along with the other 681 competitors from every corner of the state, took part in the annual Victory Dance last night in the Sugarbarn.

He brought his gray suede shoes and his best suit with him and danced until they put the lights out at 10 o'clock.

"I'm a good cook, too," said Tommy. "You ought to try my chili."

He is very special.

Working with Tommy is Tom Keller, the manager of his group home, and Dan Souheaver, the administrator. They teach him well.

"I keep my room clean, I do my own laundry, I cook my own dinner and I … uh … I — this is, sometimes I even do the dishes."

Love?

Yes, plenty of it … on the long trail from Mt. Clemens to Mackinaw City, where "Wertz Warriors" are making much of this possible. But, also in the heart of Tommy Strauss, who said: "I hope I can be a volunteer some day so I can help people out in the Special Olympics."

Sunday, February 13, 1983

Disabled — Snowfari's champions

PART V: THE GREAT SNOWFARI

MACKINAW CITY, MICH. — It was late yesterday afternoon, and the sky was gray and a soft snow was falling when here they came, down Nicolet, riding on the shoulder of the road, lights blazing, on the final leg of their long journey — 45 misty-eyed men on their snowmobiles.

From the side of the road, you could see their tears — even through their goggles — as they rumbled along in single file, carrying a group of Special Olympians on their sleds through the final mile of their 625-mile trip.

Mission: Accomplished.

This is what they came for — to help Michigan's handicapped citizens … and last night Vic Wertz, leader of this wild ride from Mt. Clemens to Mackinaw City, turned over a $65,000 check to the Michigan Special Olympics. He had been shooting for $35,000.

"I don't know when I've been more proud of anything in my life," said Wertz, the bald-headed beer baron who organized this Snowfari a year ago, when he raised $26,000.

"These men were just great. They drove long, and they drove hard, and they never got out of hand," said Wertz. "We didn't have one discipline problem all along the way."

As they stopped on a hill overlooking Mackinaw City — their long-awaited destination — Wertz shouted out: "Who's going next year?"

And 45 fists were thrust into the air, and 45 voices called out: "We are!"

It turned out to be a bittersweet journey for 'Wertz's Warriors." One of their colleagues was seriously injured along the way — Ed Palenkas Sr., 57, the man with the mustache who had awakened them with his duck calls in the morning and had kept them awake all through the day with his humor and his hugs.

Palenkas slammed into a tree just outside of Atlanta and suffered multiple injuries, including a broken leg, a broken collarbone and a concussion. He was taken to the Otsego County Memorial Hospital — the same place he was rushed to at the end of last year's ride when he suffered from kidney stones. Late yesterday afternoon, he was listed in fair but stable condition in the intensive care unit.

The mishap occurred on a back road about five miles out of Atlanta as his sled became airborne and slammed into a tree. Palenkas was knocked unconscious, and his sled was demolished.

Another sled was put down, and Marv Claeys, who'd been driving the fuel truck, finished out the ride in Ed Palenkas' name.

The mishap cast a melancholy spell over the caravan, but on they went — determined to complete the six-day sojourn.

So many good things happened:

West Branch — the Miller Beer people were doing much of the driving, but when they encountered trouble outside of West Branch, the Budweiser man in town, Bob Griffin, took them in and fed them cold cuts and hot chili and — uh — asked if anybody would like to have a Bud.

Kalkaska — A woman (who refused to give her name except to say it was Mrs. Church) having breakfast at a roadside diner when the caravan rolled into the parking lot. She said she'd seen pictures of them in the Free Press. A Detroit News man said he'd put five bucks into the pot if she'd switch papers. "Oh, I couldn't do that," she exclaimed, but put five bucks in anyway, in honor of Glenn Johnson, a Special Olympian she knew in South Boardman.

In Gaylord, just when it seemed they were getting lost on the way to Alpena, they broke out into an open field, and there, to their utter astonishment, was a roaring campfire, hot coffee and doughnuts, courtesy of the local undertaker, Don Green.

When they got to Alpena, the Holiday Inn manager, Wayne Lee, thanked the drivers for their efforts — then charged only five bucks apiece for their rooms.

In Alpena, the caravan had to switch routes from Alpena to Mackinaw City because of snow conditions, so two men from the Cheboygan County Sheriff's office — Sgt. Mike Rogers and Deputy Rod Vockel — spent the entire night riding around in the woods, from midnight to 8 a.m. staking out a new trail.

In Mackinaw City, finally, let's not forget the efforts of Gary Paja of the support team. He handled all the baggage and didn't lose a one. As the self-styled "Polish Prince" put it: "We're not like the airlines ... where you have breakfast in Detroit, lunch in Los Angeles and baggage in Brazil."

This is the last article in this series but not the end of this story.

CHAPTER 3

Organization and Fund-Raising

While the first rides were obviously quite successful, as the Wertz Warriors have grown and their goals have changed, the need for organization and participation has increased. The group is not simply a group of guys who meet up and go for a ride together; it is a well-run group of numerous volunteers with specific tasks and positions. The governing structure of the organization is a Board of Directors. There is a chairperson and members-at-large. Each member has specific responsibilities related to the goals and objectives of the organization.

The Wertz Warriors have only one paid staff person. Currently, this person is Sue DiGiorgio. Her title is Administrative Coordinator and she works part-time out of an office located at 44485 Gratiot Ave., Clinton Township, Michigan 48036. The secretary before Sue was Mary Lang who took the job in 1995 and says, "I wouldn't trade this job for anything in the world. I couldn't be prouder of these guys than I am at the opening ceremonies of Winter Games. You'd think I was their mother!"

The secretary before Mary was Pam Melby who was Vic Wertz's office manager. She served as secretary-treasurer from the beginning in 1982 to 1995. Pam did a great job and was well-liked. Rita Rosek was a tireless worker for the Warriors. She went on numerous rides as did Pam. Rita was very active in fund-raising, especially working with Digger O'Dell at the Selfridge Air National Guard Base.

Warriors who have served as chairmen of the board are Vic Wertz; a committee of four in 1984 composed of George Kavanagh, Ken Hintz, Ken Baker, and Mitch Cohoon; Ken Baker was chairman for a number of years; he was followed by Tony Pype and now Vic Battani, who has been the chairman for the past several years. There is no limit on the amount of time a chairman can serve, but the chair is elected each year by the board members.

The financial structure of the group is, of course, very important. The budget pie is cut into five pieces:

1. The administrative support of the organization is approximately 10% of all income. This pays for the secretary, office expenses, and expenses incurred on the endurance ride.

2. The organization puts an amount of money aside for grants which can be applied for by any area in the Michigan Special Olympics System.

3. The organization pays the complete direct costs of the Michigan Special Olympics Winter Games.

4. The organization returns 25% of any Warriors fund-raising when the Warrior fund-raising event happens in an area. Conversely, if no fund-raising activity occurs in an area, no money goes to the area.

5. The organization maintains a Restricted Fund and left-over dollars go to this fund, meaning if they raise more money than is needed to fund the winter games. The purpose of the Restricted Fund is to support the Winter Games if the Wertz Warriors Organization should ever cease to be. This fund is invested in the hope that the money there will grow through a strategic investment program.

Digger O'Dell says with much pride, "We know where every nickel goes. Our organization, with the exception of our administrative coordinator, is all volunteer. No one is paid, there are no benefits. It's amazing what people do when they believe in the cause."

FUND-RAISING

The whole purpose of the Wertz Warriors, besides having fun snowmobiling, is to raise money for Special Olympics Michigan. The funds are raised in two ways: First by the Warriors who must raise a dollar amount to even be a part of the endurance ride and second by the people who own bars or service organizations where the Warriors stop during their sojourn to Mackinaw City.

How do the Warriors raise the $3,500 per man that is needed in order to participate in the endurance ride? The following are fund-raisers reported by the Warriors. This is only a partial list! In many cases there are duplications and the activity is only listed once: Golf outing, turkey fries, pig roasts, auctions, bowling, car shows, begging, motorcycle raffle, motorcycle rides, Red Wing Alumni vs. Wertz Warriors hockey game, donations through customers from work, dinner with a silent auction, donations from family and friends, donations from patrons, small bass fishing tournaments, wild game dinner, poker run on Lake St. Clair, selling signs on trailers, night golf outing, golfing on the ice, 50-50 drawings and raffles, bowling party and asking a few friends and relatives who can donate $100 or so, fellow employees and employers, donations by the church on the Thursday of the ride, Frosty Invitational Golf Outing on the Ice of Sand Lake Using Numbered Tennis Balls.

> *"That's the real story, the variety of people who raised all this money!"*
>
> — *Mark Fidrych.*

Every Warrior fund-raiser is unique and valuable and like non other, but a few are presented below as rather unique efforts. Many others are noted in Chapter IX.

Donald "Digger" O'Dell had a spaghetti dinner at the Selfridge Air National Guard Base and took in $16,200.00 the first year. Each year since then, the spaghetti dinner is held from 11:30 a.m. to 10:00 p.m. in January. They have taken in as much as $32,000.00, but Digger boasts of a average of $25,000 a year. And, he has been hosting this dinner for 24 years! And, the tickets that were $12.00 in 1983, are still $12.00 in 2006. Digger thanks the Zacarro family for hosting this fund-raiser at their Banquet and Catering Center. Every year the people come back to help Digger and the Wertz Warriors.

Kevin Lee says his most important fund-raiser is a pie sale. His wife and granddaughter hand-pick apples together, make the pies and sell them for Special Olympics Michigan. One year they raised $500.00 and at $12.00 a pie, that is a lot of pies!

Steve Peters puts on a "Goofy Golf Outing." The outing is only 9 holes but there are different challenges at each hole such as the doughnut hole where golfers must tee up on a jelly doughnut and they get to take a stroke off their score if they eat the dough-nut afterwards.

Warrior Bert Sissons summarized how an idea to raise his $3,000 required to ride got started. "I started out by contacting friends, family, Christmas card list and businesses with my hand out. The first year I got a little over $3,000. As I approached my second year (1996), I got the idea to put on my own mini Wertz Warrior ride. It would be a one-day ride in the Houghton Lake area where I had a condo and was familiar with the trails. I would invite all of my snowmobile friends, charge them money, lead the ride and treat them to lunch. Lacking a place to park more than a couple of snowmobile trailers, I went down to Spicer's Boat City. Spicer's is a local boat and snowmobile store about two miles from my condo. I knew Jeff Boyd, service manager at that time, so I started with him. I asked if we could park about twenty trailers at their place and since it was a charity ride, would they be interested in starting us out with a cup of coffee? Jeff liked the idea but said that I should think bigger. He helped me expand the idea. I wrote it up and he presented it to Bob Spicer, the owner. Bob loved it! He said Spicer's did a number of promotions in the summer relative to boats and he was thinking about how they could get involved in the winter with snowmobiles. This was perfect. "Spicer's Winter Tour" was born.

"The tour included a reception on Thursday evening and an all-day event on Friday. Friday started out with coffee and donuts (later expanded to a full breakfast) at Spicer's during registration. Everyone got a commemorative hat and a Special Olympics pin at registration. Then we rode. We had three levels of groups (casual, moderate and advanced) to satisfy all skill levels. The total ride was about 90 miles long and featured stops for coffee and donuts at the Elbow Lake Bar (no alcohol), lunch at "Camp Winter Tour" on the Muskegon River and a dinner and awards ceremony in a local hall after.

"Camp Winter Tour consisted of two large heated tents — one with warm porta-johns, the other with a catered lunch of soup, chili, hot dogs, chips, coffee, pop, and all the trimmings. There was also a huge bonfire and plenty of chairs for the riders. The first year we had about 70 riders and raised over $8,000.00. The event has been held every year since and has grown to approximately 200 riders raising over $20,000.00. The total raised from 1996 through 2003 is over $131,000.00 for Special Olympics."

The feeling you get when you see those athletes, parents, coaches, and chaperones at the Winter Games is indescribable. You can see where your effort and the efforts of all donations go. I wish every donor could experience the Winter Games and see the smiles on the athlete's faces, and then get hugs and handshakes from them. The donors sure could understand and have an appreciation for what their money is doing."

— Ken Maly

While discussing possible fund-raising ideas with Kevin Lee at a stop at Ma Deeters in Luzerne, Michigan, he said with a chuckle, "We've been in so many bathrooms on these rides. I should rank them all, write a book, and sell it for ten bucks. That would be one unique fund-raiser."

Dick DeLange mentioned that the Detroit Red Wings Alumni Association has been involved, but not as riders. Alex Delvecchio and Ted Lindsay have presented checks, and been supportive of the Wertz Warriors.

At each stop along the ride, the Warriors pick up checks that are the culmination of fund-raisers throughout the year put on by service organizations, schools, retailers, churches. At each stop following the presentation of the check or the amount of money raised, honorary chairman of the ride, Mark Fidrych expresses thanks on behalf of the Warriors and presents a most attractive and personalized plaque.

The plaques are the work of Jim Hadd, the owner of Quick-Made Trophies, yet another member of the team. Jim is a big supporter of the Wertz Warriors and has been engraving the approximately 300 plaques required for each ride since the Warriors started honoring their sponsors with the attractive recognition award. Jim funds everything from September to April or May and asks payment for only the cost of the materials. One hundred and fifty are taken on the ride and given to every sponsor who donates $1,000.00 or more. Another one hundred and fifty are ordered by the riders based on the contributions received from their sponsors.

An important source of income for the Wertz Warriors in their fund-raising efforts is the selling of Wertz Warrior memorabilia. This has been the responsibility of Warrior Tim Kavanagh since 1997. In the early years there was no 'memorabilia support crew' since there was no memorabilia to sell. It wasn't until 1987 when a small amount of memorabilia in the form of a few hats and pins began to be sold on the trip. Even then no one person was relegated to the task of selling the merchandise, but instead it was performed by whoever had the time. Generally the memorabilia was placed in the luggage truck, command, or other vehicle as there wasn't enough merchandise to warrant a separate truck.

As the trip grew in size and the Wertz Warrior's community support grew, it became clear that more was needed. Around 1990, a person was tasked with ensuring that memorabilia was brought in to as many stops as possible. Often this entailed grabbing a handful of hats, pins and a few sweatshirts and placing them on a table and then waiting for someone to make a purchase.

By 1994 the amount of memorabilia to be sold grew from several hundred dollars worth to several thousand. While this was a good sign for business, it presented problems in transporting since there was no one place to put a dozen boxes of merchandise. Boxes of merchandise were hauled into bars, restaurants, Moose lodges and various other stops across the state and then sold by the assigned Warrior. By the middle of the trip, the merchandise was a mess and finding a specific sweatshirt in a given size and style was nearly impossible. Add to this the fact that the memorabilia had to be set up, sold and repacked into multiple vehicles that often took 15 minutes or more — something the Warriors could ill afford — in order to stay on time for the next stops.

In 1997 Tim Kavanagh joined the Warriors and was asked to handle all of the memorabilia. After his first trip, it was clear to him that the entire area of memorabilia needed to be completely overhauled. First he requested — and received — a large truck in which to haul the merchandise and another person to assist him. He then revamped the type, quality and amount of merchandise to be sold and contracted with a new clothing vendor (Signature Sports and Promotion, located in Mt. Clemens, Michigan) to handle most of the clothing, embroidery and screen work, and works with artists to develop new logos and artwork to be placed on clothing items. He even went so far as to create the Wertz Warriors Website (www.wertzwarriors.org) that is still in use today and enables purchases of Warrior memorabilia online!

> *"I wish all donors to Wertz Warriors and Special Olympics would have the opportunity to see the smiles on the faces of the athletes. They would see their contribution bringing joy to hundreds of athletes."*
>
> — *Fred Tate*

Finally the problem of setting up 'shop' and packing after each of the 25 or more stops quickly needed to be addressed. So he did what stores do: Hung the merchandise on clothing racks and wheeled them in and out of each location. After all, 70% of all sales are made by women on the ride so, why not make them feel like they are in a store?

The difference is the racks he uses are relatively light-weight, portable, and have large wheels. "No more boxes!" Tim proclaims. For most stops a 'staging' rack is kept on the truck and a 'sales' rack is rolled into what is largely now a designated 'sales area' at each stop. For large stops, both racks of clothing are used. A large duffel bag is used to bring in non-clothing items like baseballs autographed by Wertz Warriors Honorary Chairman Mark "The Bird" Fidrych, lanyards, hats, decks of cards, and a myriad of other memorabilia.

Set-up and re-pack time: about 3 minutes each! Tim says, "We now sell about $15,000 of Wertz Warrior, merchandise per year. Like in any business, some years are better than others."

The most popular item? "That would be the sweatshirts, hands down. Although newer clothing items such as dress shirts are also becoming much more popular," Tim explains. If you are wondering if the popular Wertz Warriors jacket is sold, absolutely not, the Green Jacket is only to be worn by the Warriors or those few who have been given the green jacket as a token of appreciation for some well-deserved contribution to the organization.

Tim has a good understanding of what is really at work in the Wertz Warriors experience. "This grounds you!" Tim says. "People get so wrapped up in the minutia of their lives — stress of their job, family and a variety of activities. They lose perspective. They lose a focus on what is really important. The Wertz Warriors experience grounds you!"

Tim went on to offer an interesting thought, "It's all a matter of perspective. A kid with a lot of problems, can't see, can't hear, etc., but he has the basics, he can respond to a touch or a smile. The fascinating thing is he doesn't realize he has a problem. In reality we have the problem." Tim has a screensaver at work and the picture is of a Special Olympics athlete. Tim says, "I look at the picture when I think I have a problem and quickly realize that I don't have any problems."

Referring to the Warriors who raise money and take a week of their lives to devote to the cause, Tim says, "It takes a certain ilk (breed) to do this."

CHAPTER 4

Who Are These Warriors?

Becoming a Wertz Warrior is also an investment in itself. You don't simply sign up. When a Warrior is chosen to ride, the decision also impacts the Warrior's family. There is sacrifice by those who remain home. However, says Sue Tomenello, wife of member Larry Tomenello, "I'm looking forward to the day when I can take Michael (their young son) to the Opening Games at the Special Olympics Winter Games. I want him to see what his father has committed himself to for all these years."

Yet it is not always an easy decision. At one point during the 2003 ride Warrior John Walker was missing his three-week-old adopted daughter and mentioned that in addition to the new baby his wife Joy was also caring for her mother who was ill. John told Joy that if she wanted him home to just say so and he would stay, no question about it, but she encouraged him to go. John was talking with Joy on his cell phone and I asked to speak with her. "I understand you're home caring for your mother and three-week-old baby and yet you support John going on this week's event." "Absolutely!" she responded. "I fully support him

— it is a great cause. The guys enjoy it and do a wonderful job for Special Olympics!"

Becoming a Wertz Warrior begins with a letter explaining why the rider wishes to become a member. The letter should explain the candidate's experience in riding a snowmobile, including how long he has ridden. Experience in helping charities is also recommended. The next step is to be sponsored by an existing member-in-good-standing. A current Wertz Warrior must vouch for the candidate and, if accepted, is responsible for the rider on the first ride.

There is a waiting list, so every snowmobiler who wishes to join is not automatically invited. Also, to be a Warrior, the invited participant must now raise a minimum of $3,500.00 in order to be eligible for the ride. Candidates not accepted are kept on file for future consideration.

Once accepted, it is not assumed that the Warrior is welcomed for all future rides. Each year the Board determines who will get a letter of invitation to go on the next ride. If a former Warrior does not get a letter, he probably should not ask why. Chances are the reasons are rooted in embarrassing the Green Jacket or the Wertz Warrior Organization either by behavior or not following the rules and regulations.

A member of the Board of Directors is responsible for processing the letters from prospective riders, obtaining sponsorship commitments from sponsors and sending the candidates copies of the organization's rules, regulations, and by-laws.

Every year one or more rookies joins the Warriors. There is a price to pay for being a rookie on the trip. Things seem to happen to sleds at various stops. The first sign of potential difficulty was a statement made by Mark Fidrych when he said to the rookies, "Have fun this week — you WILL be tormented."

INITIATION FOR ROOKIES

Mark makes this strong prediction because there is a hazing that takes place throughout the ride. Rookies are initiated in a variety of ways. For example, as the riders left a stop for another section of the ride, ROOKIE stickers could be seen plastered on the windshields of first-timers. These were transparent, except for the letters and stayed on for the duration of the ride. At another stop, more stickers appeared and at one stop, saran wrap was wrapped around a couple of rookie sleds. In Gaylord, a rookie came out of the bar only to find his sled on top of a dumpster.

Each Warrior is given a Wertz Warrior jacket that is green with yellow trim and lettering. The green jacket puts all Warriors and support crew on the same playing field. A rookie soon realizes that he must never be without the green jacket, for if a senior rider is able to take the jacket, getting it back can be quite an ordeal, either in getting it down from a tree or flag pole or having to buy it back in an auction. Some rookies take their jackets and hide them during the ride so as not to fall victim to a prank.

A rookie speech is required at the Lewiston stop telling the community and the senior riders what the ride means to them. Of course, there is the general low-life treatment and senior riders telling rookies to get a variety of items at various stops. When rookies are asked about the harassment, they all take it in stride realizing it is all part of the fun ... fun they can have next year when new Warriors join the ride.

When the rookies give their speech, some of the senior Warriors can tell which of the rookies understand the purpose of the ride and being a Wertz Warrior. Some may only be in this for themselves and it is important to realize that this is about service to others and giving to athletes. What follows are some quotes from the rookie speeches during the 2003 ride that express overall what the Warriors collectively feel:

Scott Bird: *"This is an incredible experience, to do what we are able to do and to help the athletes, plus it is a lot of fun."*

Charlie Lang: *"The amount of money these little communities raise is fantastic! The Opening Ceremonies at Winter Games are incredible."*

Rich DeLange: *"I've wanted to be a part of this experience for a long time. The Opening Ceremony at the Winter Games was unbelievable."*

Ryan Yakaboski: *"The Wednesday stop (Opening Ceremonies of Winter Games in Traverse City) is what the ride is all about. I and some others spent some time after the ceremonies interacting with the athletes. I had to wear the Warrior King hat and the kids loved it — it was a lot of fun."*

Rick Hawk: *"This is a great group of guys. Wednesday was really cool. It shows you what it's all about."*

Ken Mally: *"I thought before the ride, it's not going to happen — 900 miles in 7 days. I didn't think we'd go faster than 35 miles per hour. Before the opening ceremonies we took the athletes for rides and they loved it. If we didn't do this (ride and fund-raising) the athletes wouldn't have this opportunity. It brings tears to your eyes; it did for me when we handed them the check and the crowd went wild."*

Mike Davis: *"Yesterday (Wednesday in Traverse City) makes it all worthwhile — makes you speechless. I hope I can do this for a long time."*

Clearly, these Warriors got it, they understand what the ride is all about.

THE GREEN JACKET

Each Wertz Warrior is presented with a green jacket once he has been accepted into the organization. The jacket came into be-ing, according to Digger O'Dell, in the 4th year. The third year they all had blue jackets with white lettering. Kenny Hintz picked the green and yellow colors. Warriors wear their jackets during the ride and at all fund-raisers that they sponsor or attend. The first name or a nickname appears in the upper left front of the jacket. On the back are the words "Wertz Warriors," a picture of a snowmobile and rider with the words, "Since 1982."

The green jacket appears to be the "uniform" of the Warriors. It is a prize possession and like a uniform most are "decorated" with patches or pins given to them at the Winter Games by the athletes. Down the left sleeve are year patches signifying how many years the wearer has been on a ride either as a rider or as a member of the support crew. There is a patch for charter members who made the first ride in 1982, and a patch for a lifetime member. A lifetime member is a Warrior who has participated in rides for 15 years.

Digger O'Dell noted that at one time there was discussion of the support crew wearing a different color jacket. Digger recalled a passionate speech to the Board, "We're either all one in this effort or we aren't. You (referring to the riders) aren't going anywhere without the support crew and vice versa." The concept of different jackets was dropped. To this day, riders and support crew wear the green jacket with pride.

The American flag appears on the right sleeve with the stars of the flag toward the outside. The jacket might have a variety of patches signifying milestones of the Special Olympics Winter Games, anniversaries, for example.

The green jacket commands respect by all who know of the efforts of the Warriors. The athletes at Winter Games often come up to Warriors to get an autograph or to give a hug or a hand-shake. Charlie "Tuna" Peyerk says, "You wear this green coat up here and we're heroes; downstate, they don't know who we are."

Photographer Bob Sassanella adds, "The people up here (stops along the ride) really like to see the green jackets come into town. They really have an affinity with these people. People enjoy the men and they look forward to seeing the Wertz Warriors."

It is indeed an honor to be accepted to be a Warrior, an honor not to be taken lightly, for the wearer of the green jacket signifies a man chosen from among his peers to be capable of the endurance ride and having a heart of compassion for the athletes of Special Olympics Michigan. It is also a process that is based on inclusion and acceptance, not just a hard-core interest in riding itself.

HONORARY RIDE CHAIRMAN MARK FIDRYCH

Famous Detroit Tigers pitcher Mark "The Bird" Fidrych has been the Honorary Chairman of the ride since 1994. As he tells how he got involved, he told of being at a Celebrity Duck Hunt in Texas. He was approached by Larry King, a Wertz Warrior, and

Bob Ernst. Larry and Bob asked Mark if he'd ever thought about snowmobiling, and would he like to help out the Wertz Warriors.

"I don't know how to ride a snowmobile," Mark said.

"The guys will teach you," Larry responded.

"I'll try it, but I don't have a sled."

"We'll get one for you," Larry replied.

Fred Duemling loaned Mark his first sled, a Polaris 440. To this day, a sled is always provided for Mark to ride. In 2003 his sled became disabled and had to be hauled in. At the final ceremony, Mark was quite apologetic about being on the sled when whatever happened, happened.

Mark was asked why he comes to Michigan every year, takes a week of his life away from home (Massachusetts) to do this ride. "It's for the kids, the athletes. It is all about giving back. They were there at the ball parks for me — you give back."

In his role as honorary chairman of the ride, Mark presents a plaque to those who have raised thousands of dollars for Special Olympics. He also speaks at opening ceremonies at the Winter Games in Traverse City. Mark is a gentleman, always has a smile and is willing to shake hands and sign autographs for fans of all ages.

CHAPTER 5

Aspects of the Ride

The organization has four semi-trailers which have been designed for transporting sleds and one serves as a "garage." The remaining three have cabs which are donated by others and are driven by licensed and experienced semi-trailer drivers. In 2003 the drivers were Dave Piprzak. Joe Baker, Dave Beecherl, and Bob May. All of the sleds and support vehicles are owned by Wertz Warriors members or have been donated by Ford or Chrysler Corporation.

The snowmobile, like any piece of equipment, has improved in its design and operating potential. In the early years of the endurance run, many sleds would break down but over the years, the machines have improved significantly. In 2003 there were four well-known manufacturers. These are, in alphabetical order: Arctic Cat, Polaris, Ski-Doo, and Yamaha. The most popular sled on the ride is Arctic Cat which accounts for about half of the sleds.

The typical sled can go about 110 miles with 11 gallons of gasoline. Speeds on the trails vary but average around 50 mph with sleds going quite fast on straightaways and slower on trails with many turns or over rough terrain. Warrior Ned "Trust me" Cavallaro explained his sled in the following way, "I have a 2000 model Polaris. It has adjustable suspension (hard or soft), heated handlebars, a two-stroke engine that gives 90-175 horsepower. It has an oil-injected system and as the engine runs, it shifts power to a crankshaft that has a variable belt drive. This drives the track which propels the sled forward." Don Maes says, "These new machines are like being shot out of a gun and riding a Cadillac!"

For the less than sophisticated reader the sled can be explained this way. Every sled but one in the 2003 ride was a two-stroke (two-piston) engine and a mixture of gas and oil is fed to the piston valve that, when given a spark by the spark plug, fires and this moves the piston up and down. The movement of the piston, attached to the crankshaft, turns the belt-driven system which then transfers the power to the track. The track is circular under the sled (front to back) and it is the friction of the track on the snow/ground that moves the sled forward.

The engines in the snowmobiles are cooled by anti-freeze but, unlike a car, the snowmobile has no radiator. The engine is cooled by the movement of anti-freeze through long-range chambers that circle the sled. All the sleds have heat exchangers and in 98% of them, above the track are coolers built into the chassis of the snowmobile. Cooling happens when the cold snow is whirled around the coolers which contain the anti-freeze.

Jay Dixon pointed out that a snowmobile needs snow to keep the sleds cool and to create the lubricant to keep the sliders from melting. The sliders are underneath the track. The snow keeps the sliders cool and provides a lubricant. If the sled is driven too long on a surface that isn't snow-covered or covered, but not sufficiently, the sliders will melt and lock the sled. In addition, the engine will overheat and be damaged. This is why the snowmobile needs to be on sufficient snow. The riders obviously like a good base of snow, but have to ride on what is available and sometimes as in crossing a road, ride on pavement.

The Warrior is also passionate about his sled, knows what it can do, and often pushes it to its limits. There is a demeanor of cockiness that is sometimes present. "We're Warriors, we don't need snow," says Willie Brandon.

"We make new limits. We're riding for the athletes, we push the sleds," says T.J. Grunwald. "We know the limits and how far we can push it."

The equipment required to outfit a typical participant is no less involved than the structure of the snowmobile, and equally important. The safe and warm rider looks like an astronaut heading to the shuttle for a trip into space. The following was described by Warrior Rob Carter as equipment and approximate costs (these will vary for a number of reasons, but are presented here to give the reader an idea of what the rider uses for equipment. Also, these costs are based on prices in 2003):

1. Pair of Gloves — $40-50

2. Pair of Boots — $100

3. Bibs — $100

4. Coat — $80-90

5. Helmet — $125

6. Face Mask (worn under the helmet) — $15

This — along with a sled that can cost anywhere from $6,000 to $10,000, $500 for carbide studs (required in the track of all Wertz Warriors sleds), $80.00 for a set of carbide rail bars, $45.00 a piece for sliders, and 2-3 belts at $60.00 a pair — prepares the rider for the outdoors. In addition, once the rider has a sled, basic replacement parts, and clothing/safety apparel and is ready to ride in the event, there are still additional costs. Overall, participation is a substantial individual commitment in itself. Added to the above costs must be licenses and insurance.

PRE-RIDE ACTIVITIES

There is a set preparation before each ride can begin based for one on a commitment to safety and, in a sense, tradition.

PHYSICAL EXAM. Each rider must have a physical exam which is offered by Dr. David Mandy, himself a current member of the Special Olympics Michigan Board and the father of three Special

Olympics athletes. David, who has given free physicals for the past 12 years, is assisted by his wife Jane who does all of the paperwork. Dr. Mandy indicated that only one Warrior has been directed not to ride because of health. That rider took the doctor's advice and has since thanked Dr. Mandy for discovering a major threat to his health. That rider has been able to resume rides since the evaluation. In connection with the physical, each rider must provide health information which is filed and kept by the commander. If medical attention is needed during the ride, the commander will give to the paramedic or attending physician all the medical information on hand for the injured rider.

SLED INSPECTION. Each sled must undergo an inspection to make sure it is safe and meets all rules set by the Wertz Warriors Organization. The sleds are inspected by Tom May, the chief mechanic for the organization. Also checked are the registrations required of every sled.

BREAKFAST AND BLESSING. The riders and support crew all gather at Zuccaro's for a full breakfast buffet provided free of charge to the Warriors. This tradition began in 1986. A member of the clergy, Ralph Leach, Chaplain for St. Joseph Hospital, offers a blessing on the Warriors. The caravan then begins to head north to the first stop where, if sufficient snow exists, the ride begins. Since 1985, the first stop and the demarcation point for the endurance ride has been Skidway Lake which is north and east of Bay City.

ROUTES

The routes traveled are not random; there is a committee for this as well. In the summer, the Warrior who will lead the route on a day inspects the entire route. The Board of Directors approves the routes which are then shared with the chairman of the support crew so he can become familiar with the area, and highlighting county maps.

Each day of the ride, one or more Warriors is designated to be the Route Leader and this is because the men so chosen know the area. The route leader can make a change due to circumstances. Needless to say, the responsibility of the route leader is awesome.

Tony Pype speaks for the Warriors in expressing his appreciation for the route leaders. "I would like to thank the route leaders we have had through the years, because without them we would have no trail memories to talk about, as in missed turns where Fred Duemling got his nickname 'Splash,' or Jack Conner leading us into a garbage dump, or the Howard "Duck" Redd taking us through a logging area that had turned into mud, or Bill Freeham taking us on a shortcut across a lake 3 foot-deep in slush in the dark, or Carl 'I know the way' Hart taking us to view gas wells on the way to Lewiston. Or, 'Turn Around' Ternes showing us who we really are on the trail. All kidding aside, these guys donate extra time and money to make the ride a success and we all owe them a great deal for their extra effort."

There is one trail of the 900 plus miles the Warriors seek to cover that must be mentioned. The Wertz Warrior Trail has been named by the state of Michigan in honor of the Warriors. The trail parallels I-75 on the west side of the highway between the Grayling northbound exit and 4 Mile Road. A sign is posted naming the trail, and if you glance to the west going south on I-75 in the dead of winter, you may see some snowmobiles on the Wertz Warrior Trail, a fine tribute to the selfless giving to others which is the trademark of the Warriors.

1. Macomb
2. Skidway Lake
3. Sand Lake
4. Houghton Lake
5. Leota
6. Lake City
7. Mesick
8. Kalkaska
9. Grayling
10. Lost Creek
11. Clear Lake
12. St. Helen
13. Silver Dollar
14. Grayling
15. Swamp
16. Kihootees
17. Traverse City
18. Mancelona
19. Alba
20. Lovells
21. Lewiston
22. Elbow
23. Lakes of the North
24. Jake's Place
25. Petoskey
26. Chateau Lodge
27. Hawks
28. Gaylord

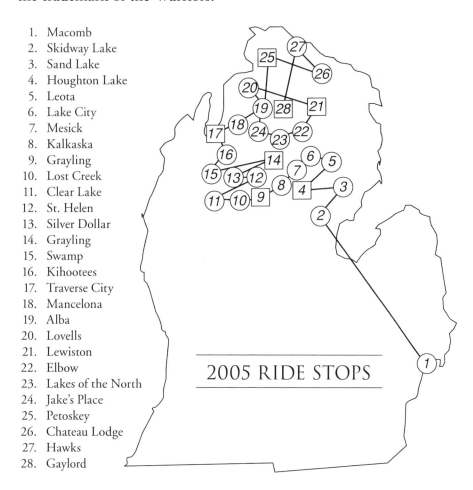

2005 RIDE STOPS

COMMUNICATION

As noted elsewhere there are four sleds with radios: one in front, one in back, and two in the middle. There is a paramedic within the riders who is positioned somewhere in the middle of the pack. The paramedic is Ted May who in real life is a paramedic. He also has a radio so he can learn of any problem ahead or behind him.

Vic Battani, chairman of the board of directors for the Wertz Warriors, is the rider of the backup sled. He is always the last sled and assures that all riders have gone before him.

The sleds are all numbered from one to the last registered sled. For the most part the riders have a say in what number they wish based on where they would like to ride. Early in the tour, the Warriors are asked to, as much as possible, stay in the order of their numbers. The sleds for the most part move in single file but like the Indianapolis 500 or a NASCAR event, there is some jockeying for position, some tapping of sleds, and some shortcuts that may be taken in the course of the ride.

Experienced riders will tell you that concentration and focus has to be 100% because the trail changes and the snow dust (the snow that sleds in front kick up) create a visual handicap. The rider must always know that snow dust means that another rider is either there or has been there recently. There is little time for enjoying the scenery. The rider is concentrating on the trail in front of him, what is happening around him, and managing his sled. This is not a pleasure ride, even though it is a lot of fun; it is an endurance ride to cover hundreds of miles and to do so safely.

Once the ride is underway, two communication systems are used. The central point of communication is the command vehicle, a motor home. The commander in 2003 was John Beecherl. He has two microphones. One is used to communicate with the 4 sleds out on the trails that are equipped with radios. These riders are positioned at the front, back, and two are within the pack. They key in when they want to talk and can hear what is being said through a speaker in their helmet. These riders communicate with sleds that are disabled and need to be picked up. They also relay information about any accidents or problems that are encountered on the ride.

The second is used to communicate with the support vehicles that accompany the riders, but must, for obvious reasons, travel on parallel county roads. Each support vehicle — including security vehicles, the vehicle pulling surplus gasoline, each semi driver, and a number of vehicles used to retrieve disabled sleds or vehicles that are stuck — has a radio.

As the reader can imagine, the command center operates much like an air traffic control tower at an airport. The commander needs to monitor the progress or lack thereof of the caravan of sleds and needs to monitor the movement of all support vehicles, directing them where to go. The commander has a detailed county map so as to know all roads in the area, as well as the snowmobile route that is being used by the riders.

The man behind the radio communication system is the driver of the command vehicle, Bob Brockett. Bob joined the Wertz Warriors at the request of Digger O'Dell, who was Bob's neighbor and who knew of Bob's interest and talent with radios. Bob was a ham radio operator and has specialized knowledge and skill that have been useful in designing an effective communication system between the command vehicle and the sleds and support crew members.

Before Bob had designed the radio system in use today, it was difficult at best to keep track of snowmobile movement and problems that riders encountered. One year, Digger O'Dell, who was the commander at that time, rode in a small plane to keep track of snowmobile movement. He recalled seeing a bad accident when Ed Palenkas hit a tree head on, unable to negotiate a curve. Ed cracked his helmet open and he would have been dead had it not been for the barrier. Digger was able to contact the base command and arrange for an ambulance to be sent. At that time the Warriors took a paramedic and a doctor on the ride. These personnel helped Ed until the ambulance arrived. Needless to say, good organization played a large role in avoiding a more serious outcome to the accident.

The Wertz Warriors have a mutual respect for one another. Each member has a job to do, a responsibility, that when executed with precision allows the ride to progress safely and smoothly. The person responsible for the support crew is the commander who rides in the motor home command center.

For 11 years that commander was Digger O'Dell. Digger had retired from the Air Force in 1975. He accepted a civilian job at Selfridge Air National Guard Base as Director of Public Affairs. The Selfridge Base is the only base in the world that has all branches of the military on it.

Digger recalled getting a phone call from Vic Wertz. "What are you doing for lunch?" Vic asked. Digger responded, "Is there such a thing as a free lunch?" The two had lunch at the Cruise Inn Restaurant. Vic told Digger of the first two rides and would Digger help out by getting the Base Community Council involved. The Community Council was a group of business people who came to the base once a month for a meeting. Digger was sure he could get the military and the council to support his effort. Digger said to Vic, "Sounds like a great idea, count me in!"

Digger recalled that they had 30 days to raise money for the Warriors. They had a spaghetti dinner and took in $16,200.00 the first year. Vic supplied free beer from his distributorship. The powers that be on the base allowed military and civilian personnel to attend the fund-raiser.

In 1994 Digger said it was "time for somebody else to do this." The person to pick up the reins was John Beecherl who has served in this role for the past nine years. In 2005, Larry Tomenello became the operations chief.

John says, "Our job is to move 100 guys 200 miles a day." He points to the success of the support crew saying that every guy does the same job. When a new support Warrior comes on board he comes on to do a specific job for which he is skilled; he knows what he will do and does it.

Everything concerning daily activities goes through the command center. The support crew is composed of a variety of functionaries. The head of luggage transfer is Bob Bradley, a long-time Warrior. He is assisted by Greg Beck, Charlie Nemitz, and Karl Kasner. At each overnight stop, Warriors must bring their luggage to the door closest to the luggage van. The handlers put the bags onto the truck. They then drive to the next overnight stop and put all bags into the assigned rooms, two riders to a room. Bob also works with the motel to assign room numbers to the Warriors so that when they arrive they are given the key to their rooms.

TRANSPORTATION AND GASOLINE

There are three semis that carry the sleds to Skidway Lake, the beginning of the ride and carry the sleds whenever the chairman decides that conditions are not adequate for the ride. One of the semi drivers is Warrior Joe Baker, son of Ken Baker, an early leader of the Wertz Warriors. Joe has been a driver for about 5 years.

He came on board at the last minute as help was needed. Joe says, "Our job is to help — you have to be able to help these guys when they need it. You do anything they need to keep these guys going. If we're there to help them when they need it, then we're doing our job."

As the semi went down the road, Joe responded to what makes a good day for him on the ride. "Well, with any luck, it is quiet!" By this he meant, "The sleds are down and are having good snow for the ride. It is a lot of work to load the sleds onto the semis and off again when conditions warrant.

"These guys are up here to be on the sleds and snowmobile, so when these guys are on the ground snowmobiling, life is a whole lot easier."

A second driver is Warrior Dave Beecherl, son of the chairman of the command center, John Beecherl. Dave is 26 years old and is driving for the 4th year. The week with the endurance ride means a lot to this young man. He says, "I'll drive anything. If I can't drive a semi, I'll drive a support vehicle, a bus, it doesn't matter, just to see the look on the athletes' faces at Winter Games. It makes you feel important."

Dave noted that each year is different. Last year, 2002, was not a good year for snow. In fact, they didn't drop the sleds (take the sleds from the semis onto the ground) till the 5th day, which was a Friday. It was a warm period and the snow wasn't there to support the sleds until they got to the northern most reaches of the Lower Peninsula.

Dave explains that each semi can carry 18-20 sleds and that the sleds sit on two levels. The sleds are driven up ramps from the ground to the semi floor and then half are driven up a ramp to the top level. Once full, the ramp is hoisted up by pulleys and secured. Then the lower level is filled with sleds that come up a ramp and sit single file, two rows. The sleds are not secured to the semis. They have brakes on and are heavy enough that there is no movement inside the semi.

The driver of the gasoline support vehicle is Warrior Winnie Winsten. Winnie carries 250 gallons of premium gas so that he can "give a little splash" to riders who need a bit more to get them to the next gas-up. In the early days, the Warriors brought a gasoline truck with them, but it took a long time to fuel the sleds as only two hoses could be used. With the modern-day stations with multiple pumps, it is faster and more economical to use commercial stations.

Arrangements are made in advance so the proprietors know the Warriors will be coming through. The visit is anticipated as hundreds of dollars of gasoline is purchased in a matter of minutes. The amount varies with the need for gas, but can be as little as $600 to $700 to well over $1,000.00 per stop. (This is based on the price of gasoline in 2003.) The sleds are refueled at gas stations along the route. Winnie says that on a ride with good snow, the Warriors would use 7,000 gallons of gas and 1800 gallons of diesel fuel. On a good travel day, all sleds will stop 2-3 times. The sleds come into the station and line up at each pump. A member of the support crew puts gas into the sled. The driver moves on and the next sled pulls up and this goes on till the line at the pump is gone. It takes about 15 minutes for all the sleds to be fueled. If any support vehicle needs gas, the vehicle is fueled after the sleds are fueled. Once all sleds are fueled, the caravan roars off to continue the ride.

Winnie, who now lives in Florida in winter but comes north for this annual ride, was invited to join the Warriors by Digger O'Dell who called him and told him to pack clothes for a week as he was going on a trip. Winnie, who worked at Selfridge Air National Guard Base where Digger was the Public Relations Chair replied, "I've got to call my boss."

"No need to do that. I already did."

The way was clear for Winnie to go on the trip and off he went. "That first year, we left on a Sunday. That Wednesday, I knew I would never do this again in my life. Sleds were breaking down, it was very cold, and the experience was just horrible!" But then something happened that changed his attitude. "The next day at Sugar Loaf Resort was the opening ceremonies of the Special Olympics Winter Games. Once I saw that, my attitude changed and I understood what the effort was all about. I decided to help out for one more year and I'm still doing it."

When asked why he does it, Winnie responded, "I've done some good things in my life and I've done some bad things. I'm planning on this work being my ticket into Heaven — it could balance me down. Once you see the athletes smile, laugh, and having fun, you know why you do this year after year. To me, there is nothing in this world that is more exciting than seeing a child smile and laugh."

Winnie has done a lot of jobs as a member of the support crew. He has been a chase vehicle driver responsible to pick up disabled sleds, a member of the luggage team, and for many years, the driver of the gas supply vehicle. Reflecting on all the rides, he says, "I think the good Lord was looking over us on many occasions."

CHAPTER 6

Support Staff / Vehicles

The primary function of all of the support staff is, of course, safety. There are two security vehicles with a driver and a rider in each. The security vehicles are responsible to be the lead and last vehicle on the support crew. In 2003, Digger O'Dell and Bill McInnis manned the lead vehicle and Rick "Toby" Thierry and John "Buckwheat" Walker manned the last vehicle. They are responsible to stop traffic at highway crossings or at intersections in towns. The vehicles have a red flashing light that is turned on only while stopped at a crossing site and then only when the Warriors are about to or are crossing the road.

The responsibility of the chase vehicles is, when directed by the command center, to get a disabled sled. The driver and helper get to the sled and load it and move ahead. A support member in his 11th year is Warrior Harold Bevins, who was a rider for eight years.

Harold speaks of the danger in the ride, "It's a miracle that nobody's been killed. We've had some broken legs and dislocated shoulders, and some pretty serious accidents, but no life has been lost. Snowmobiles you can buy, but you can't buy life." *(note: Harold said this in 2003 before the tragic accident that took the life of Warrior Pat Modos.)*

Harold recalls that, "Guys get reckless, see how fast you can get your group through the trails." One rider has "Lucky" on his helmet and on the hood of his snowmobile. When asked why he commits his time and energy to this ride, Harold says, "When you see those athletes up there — they bring tears to your eyes. You would think we were movie stars or something. Athletes come up and say, 'We love you guys!' and give us hugs." Asked if he would continue to devote time to the Warriors, Harold says, "The only way I'd quit is if my health got so bad, I couldn't do it."

Another support vehicle driver is Charlie "Tuna" Peyerk. "Tuna" says, "The best feeling you can have is when the kids hug you and you go into opening ceremonies — if you can't feel that joy, you don't belong on this ride. All the money, all the attention is nice, but the feeling of love from the athletes is special." Tuna says any day when there are no mosquitoes is a good day on the ride.

It is not uncommon for vehicles to become stuck. The command center may call on a support vehicle with the capability of pulling vehicles out of snowbanks to do so. With today's powerful off-road, 4X4 vehicles, pulling an SUV from off the road isn't much of a chore.

One more support driver is Warrior Don Maes. Don is often called upon by John to take people where they need to go. Several years ago, Don was asked to drive Steve Foster to the Beaumont Hospital in Detroit as the local hospital was not able to adequately care for his condition. Don drove the rider down, stayed with him until he was admitted, his parents were present, and then he drove back up north to join the group, arriving around 3:00 a.m.

Not all support drivers and helpers are former snowmobilers or men who enjoy the sport with less intensity than an endurance ride. Warrior Abe Farrah, who has always been a member of the support crew, has zero interest in riding, saying, "You wouldn't get me on one of those things!" Unofficially, Digger O'Dell's wife Susie is a member of the support crew in that every year she makes about 15-20 dozen cookies to be placed in every support vehicle. Each semi-driver gets a package of cookies and the riders manage to be fed as well.

Richard "Bubba" Felix is in his 2nd year as a support crew person. Bubba was brought into the Warriors by Rick Thierry. Bubba had demonstrated commitment to charity by his work in his Lions Club for 20 years. His job this year is learning the roads, helping with sleds, and pumping gas at refueling stops. Bubba experienced Opening Ceremonies in Traverse City and exclaimed, "That opening ceremony was really something!"

THE PHOTOGRAPHERS: STILL AND VIDEO

The Warriors have an official still photographer, Bob "Sass" Sassanella. Bob began his association with the Wertz Warriors when he worked as a photographer for *The Macomb Daily*. His first trip was in 1984. He flew up in a helicopter to get photos and then flew home to get the photos in the paper. In 1985 Bob started to make the entire trip. From 1984-1988, Bob would send his photos back to *The Macomb Daily* which in turn would present daily features to their readers.

Bob would cover the snowmobile endurance ride as an employee of the paper. His photos of the trip would appear with regularity. In 1989 *The Macomb Daily* decided not to send Bob with the Warriors. He then decided to continue to accompany the Warriors on his own time and at his own expense. Other than a missed trip in 1994 due to a back operation, Bob has been on most every trip. Bob takes photos, makes 4 copies of each and puts them out for the Warriors to take, if they choose, at the annual banquet.

The official video photographer is Dave White. Dave has gone with the Warriors every year but the first year. He started in 1983. He videotaped and edited them from 1983 to 1997. One tape was a "serious" account of the ride and the second was an edited collection of memories of Warriors. Since 1997, Dave has only produced one tape. He sells his videos to Warriors and other interested persons. Dave also donates a video to each stop along the ride to promote the ride.

Dave's passion for recording and editing began as a hobby. It is now a full-time occupation. For 30 years he was a supermarket manager. Vic Wertz knew Dave through a business relationship. Vic showed Dave a video that his employees had taken the first year of the ride. When Vic learned of Dave's interest and talent in videography, he invited him to go along. Dave was the second cameraman on the second year of the ride and has gone solo since then.

Dave and Bob work as a team. Together they have captured the activity and the magical moments of the Warriors and their rides for all but the first ride. Bob specializes in photos of individuals and Dave specializes in action. At each stop they can be seen using their talent to capture interesting and significant moments of the rides.

CHAPTER 7

Classic Stories From the Past

The following is a collection of some of the more memorable moments, both good and bad, that have occurred throughout the years of the Wertz Warriors' existence.

LARRY TERNES AND THE CEMENT BRIDGE

Larry Ternes tells the story of his first ride, which was the inaugural ride in 1982. Larry was very proud of his sled saying, "The sled was my baby." The riders started from Vic's distributorship in Mt. Clemens. They soon came to a long cement bridge with no snow. Larry stopped as he was not willing to drive his sled on the snow-less concrete.

Larry King comes along, stops, and says, "What's wrong?"

"I'm not driving the sled across this bridge — this is ridiculous."

Larry King looked at Larry, gets on the snowmobile, drives it over the bridge, and then walks back to Larry. "Well, now you don't have to drive it across."

Both Larrys then walked across the bridge, got onto their sleds and continued the trip.

FRED "SPLASH" DUEMLING
GOES INTO THE MANISTEE RIVER

Fred Duemling had the fastest sled in 1987. On Tuesday coming into Houghton Lake, Fred decided to race the others to Gaylord and there was a lot of straightaway along the pipeline. He was 40th back and was determined to race to the front and become the leader. He did pass everyone but then the road cut at the Little Manistee River and Fred didn't realize it and he was going too fast to negotiate the curve. He drove his sled off the 12-14 foot bank and he landed in the ice cold river sinking about 18 inches. The word got to the other riders, "Fred's in the river!" He was pulled out with a towrope which as Fred explained was like, "Pulling up a fish." The sled was pulled out and up the bank. The sparkplugs were removed and cleaned, the sled was turned upside down to release any water inside. Fred was given some dry clothes, started the sled, and moved along to the Holiday Inn in Gaylord. His streak continued in spite of the accident.

NEIL'S BOOTS ARE ON FIRE!

Neil Foster had a favorite pair of boots. They were green with a dirty yellow stripe on the bottom. He had worn these boots for the last 15 years and according to Carl, they "were hideous, old, stinky boots." They could stand up in the corner by themselves. People were sick and tired of "Neil's stinky boots."

Roy Heisner conned Neil's roommate into getting the boots out of his room. On Friday when all were about to leave the Atlanta Eagles, Tom May placed the boots in the middle of the parking lot, poured gas on the boots, and set the boots aflame. The Warriors stood in a big circle watching Neil's boots being consumed by fire as black smoke billowed up and over the gathered crowd.

Neil saw what was happening and went wild. "What are you doing to my boots!" Neil exclaimed. All present watched the boots burn and then the left-over ashes were shoveled up and put in a garbage can. That was the end of Neil's Stinky Boots! By the way, the Warriors all chipped in and presented Neil with a new pair and he was on his way.

Larry Ternes explains, "Neil Foster was one of a kind, of which rubbed a good many people the wrong way ... but in essence he was the one who always tried to include everyone, there was always a pat on the back or a name dropped for a job well done ... his jokes and stories were always an important part of our endeavors

… and he had a tremendous ability to shine the light on all the people who took part in fund-raisers, he made them feel special and he never left them without the encouragement they needed to carry on for yet another year. Neil was a big man, with a truly big heart."

Tony Pype adds, "I met Neil the first year I went on the ride. He was one of the first-year guys. I remember being out on the trail and was having a problem with my Yamaha snowmobile. In those days there was always something going wrong with these machines, brand new or not. I remember having to stop to try and fix it. Neil pulled alongside of me to help. I took out the spark plugs to see if they were fouled. I looked at them and they seemed fine. Neil said, 'Let me see them.' He looked at them and said, 'They're bad.' He took them and threw them out into the snow. I looked at him and said, 'They weren't bad and they cost nine dollars a piece!' He looked at me and said, 'Well, they're bad now.' I proceeded to put in the new ones and we got on our way. The spark plugs didn't fix it and I was out eighteen dollars.

"Through the year I got to know Neil and figured him out. He was this great big man that seemed very rough and mean on the outside, but was this gentle giant on the inside. He was known as 'the Breeze.' Neil used to really upset people because he really cared about Special Olympics Michigan. He would always be questioning people and their ideas, but always in the best interest of Wertz Warriors and Special Olympics Michigan.

"About five or six years before Neil died, he had gotten pretty sick. That year he couldn't ride, but he'd still come with us on the trip. The day that Neil was to lead he came to me and said, 'I can't ride, you'll have to lead.' I looked at Neil and said, 'I don't remember the way you go.' He replied, 'You know, it's mostly roads and I'll lead you in my car and point you to the trail and then meet you at the next road.' Well, believe it or not it went perfectly and people were congratulating me on the good job I did as route leader.

"Neil was very important to the ride. He got the Michigan Moose Clubs involved with us and they have raised hundreds of thousands of dollars for Special Olympics through the years and are still very involved with us and we have new people picking up where Neil left off. Neil was also very instrumental in getting a lot of the northern stops to come on board like Houghton Lake, Manton, Mesick, Grayling, and Skidway Lake, just to name a few. After Neil's illness he'd say how much better he was feeling and didn't know how much longer he could ride. The year before Neil died he told me that this was the best he'd felt in years and things in his life were better than ever. Neil passed away in April of 2003 and is greatly missed but lives on through Wertz Warriors and Special Olympics Michigan."

YOU MADE MY MONTH!

In the first or second year of the ride, as the caravan pulled into Topinabee, Michigan, it was 50 below zero with the wind chill. The riders went into a bar and Vic told the bartender to put out a couple of cases of beer and whatever else the guys wanted to drink. The bartender had to get a neighbor to help him serve all of the Warriors. When they were ready to leave, Vic paid the tab and said, "Guess we made your day, huh?" The bartender replied, "Made my day? You made my MONTH!"

DETROIT TIGERS CATCHER BILL FREEHAM HAS A FURRY EXPERIENCE

Sometimes the stories are slightly less innocent. At one point, Bill Freeham, former Detroit Tigers catcher was the Honorary Chairman of the ride from 1984 to 1989. Bill would often greet the riders when they arrived at Jake's Bar in Boyne Falls. Bill had a place in Lewiston. One year, when the Warriors were in Lewiston, Bill was presented with a fur-lined jock strap made by Harold Wilcoxson's wife, Mary. Since then, Mark Fidrych has also been presented with a fur-lined jock strap.

Another tale involves Harold Wilcoxson, who was a magician and one who was always entertaining people. For many years he would escort the Warriors into town on a snowmobile wearing only boots, a leopard-skin bra and panties, and a wig under a helmet. None of the Warriors knew who this was and many were sure it was a woman!

THE MUSICIAN — "WILD BILL" WERDERMAN

Several years ago, "Wild Bill" Werderman, a member of the support crew, had a band called "Unholy Beast" and was quite an entertainer. Warriors enjoy telling the story of how Bill and others were in a bar in the Holiday Inn in Grayling where a rock and roll band was providing the entertainment. The band was not generating much enthusiasm from the patrons. Bill asked if during a break he could take the microphone and sing a song. Permission was granted and in a matter of minutes the people were having a ball. Wild Bill had captured his audience who cried for more and enjoyed the talent of the short and older man. Carl Hart recalled that, "The place was rocking."

Rick Thierry remembered another episode when the patrons were appreciative of Bill's talent and wanted to give some money. The owner of the bar said that he would match whatever the patrons contributed with the donations not going to Wild Bill but to Special Olympics. Little did the bartender realize that hundreds of dollars were put into the kitty and he matched it. More than $1,000.00 was raised for Special Olympics in that one spontaneous outburst of talent.

Another instance was a man by the name of Neil Trainor who went on some of the endurance rides strictly to entertain. He was a Johnny Cash look-alike. He dressed like Cash, carried a guitar wherever he went, and sang Johnny Cash songs.

"RIDE, WARRIORS, RIDE" AND "GO FOR THE GOLD"

"Ride Warriors Ride" was written by Matt Winans in 1990. Matt told Dave White that the Warriors could use his song for our purposes to raise money for the cause. It was recorded by Homestead Productions located in Tower, Michigan.

Matt currently lives in Florida and works as a carpenter by trade. He was inspired to write the song after watching the Warriors come into the Elbow Bar in Atlanta, Michigan, and raise money for Special Olympics Michigan. He was further inspired by watching Dave White's videos. He would occasionally sing his songs in the bar and there wouldn't be a dry eye in the place. He also wrote a song called "Go for the Gold" for the Special Olympics Michigan athletes.

GASOLINE TRUCK OUT OF CONTROL IN TRAVERSE CITY!

Digger O'Dell told the story of Marv Claeys losing control of the fuel truck on a very icy intersection on the outskirts of

Traverse City. The fuel truck didn't hit any vehicles but did go off into a field. The police came and were not very helpful or cooperative. That is, until Warrior Dick DeLange approached the officer and said, "Hey, weren't you a cop in Sterling?" The two connected and the attitude of the officer instantly changed to, "How can I help you guys?"

FROZEN EYES!

In the first or second year of the event when Vic Wertz rode a portion of the tour, an accident happened. The activity following the accident was more dangerous than the accident itself. Vic fell from his sled and cracked his face shield. An employee-friend said, "Here boss, use mine." The Good Samaritan used the cracked face shield and the ride continued. When they got to their destination, the friend-employee was blind. His eye balls had iced over like the windshield of a car. The doctor said to leave it alone and let the warmer temperatures inside take care of the problem naturally. This is what happened, but in the end the man did lose some visual acuity.

That story was told by Neil Foster while some Warriors were in the lobby of a motel in Lewiston awaiting a shuttle ride to the evening dinner/program at St. Francis Church. What was interesting was to observe the younger riders listening intently to the veteran Neil Foster telling a story of a past event. The stories get passed down and this was enjoyable to see.

CUTTING ACROSS THE LAKE — TAKING A SHORTCUT

In the days when the Opening Ceremonies were held northwest of Traverse City, the riders drove their sleds to the Sugar Loaf Resort and when the ceremonies were over, they drove their sleds back to Traverse City. The riders were advised that a shortcut that would save many minutes involved going across a lake. The advice was taken and soon the riders encountered a huge area of slush! The machines got stuck in the slush. As one can imagine, it took a long time to free each sled by hand towing the sled from the slush. So, the shortcut to save a few minutes ended up costing them a couple of hours!

Digger O'Dell fires off one of his one-liners, "The shortest distance between two points is not necessarily the best way!"

ANIMALS IN THE WAY!

Rick "Dead Horse Walking" Rheeder hit a horse on a county road just outside of Houghton Lake. Apparently there were two horses in a field (cemetery) and as the riders passed, the horses started to spook, and one of them ran alongside the fence line which was parallel to the road. Along this fence there was an opening. The horse, unfortunately, decided to go through which put animal and man on a collision course. Rick clipped it just enough to send the horse out of control. It fell to the ground with a broken leg. The authorities were notified and the idea of payment to the farmer for his loss was discussed, but he had a history of letting his animals run free so no charges or money were involved.

On another occasion, out of the corner of Larry Ternes' eye, on a bright and beautiful day, he noticed a deer busting out of the woods running on a parallel course with him. He tried to slow down to avoid it, but as it jumped down from higher ground to the road it was right beside him. He hit just enough for her to lose her balance and she collapsed on top of his hood. To this day, Larry still remembers thinking to himself how big those two brown eyes were because she was looking right at him. The force of the collision swung the rest of her body around to Larry's side and hit his leg, and he also remembers how warm it felt. As it turned out, the deer just spun around a few times, got up and ran off, and as for Larry … no damage done except for the trail of deer snot (nasal mucus) running down his hood.

COMING DOWN SUGAR LOAF MOUNTAIN

When the Opening Ceremonies were held at Sugar Loaf Resort near Cedar, Michigan, on the Leelanau Peninsula, a tradition was established whereby the Warriors would make their way to the top of the mountain and on signal would slowly descend in single file while zigzagging down to the bottom where they would ride in front of the athletes and guests who would give them a thunderous welcome. It was an awesome sight. Each snowmobile had its headlight turned on so you saw this huge "snake" slithering down the snow-covered hill. While this was going on, a colorful display of fireworks was underway and a huge Special Olympics symbol was presented on the hill.

However, Wayne Lee missed the message of how the sleds would descend. When he got to the top of the Mountain, he looked down and saw all the people at the bottom and thinking they would race to the bottom replied, "This ain't good! When we start racing someone is going to get killed!" Wayne was briefed and everyone lived.

For the reader who is not familiar with the mountain in front of the resort (at this time the resort does not exist), the mountain rises quite abruptly in front of the lodge. Warrior Bob Bradley tipped over on one of the zigzags and rolled down the hill.

Dan Schroeder recalled those Opening Ceremony descents. "One of the highlights of the ride was coming down that hill. You could hear them (athletes and guests) screaming down there." Jim Simpson recalled that it was a bit scary to perch at the top and anticipate the ride down. "It was frightening being on the top and knowing you had to go down that hill."

THE POTATO FIELD

One particular region covered in the ride has become a tra-dition unto itself. A bit north of Alba can be found acres and acres of flat farmland. This area is known as the "potato field." Permission is sought for the Warriors to ride over the snow-cov-ered land. Over the years, this long straightaway has become a place where the Warriors can race and they do, reaching amaz-ing speeds. The official race is to be 1,000 feet. But there is no of-ficial start and there is no official finishing line, so the number of Warriors who proclaim victory are numerous and the reasons for others not winning are even more numerous.

The potato field race is not without incident as whenever you mix humans, machines, and speed, something is bound to hap-pen. As the rider is fairly close to the ground, it is difficult to know where the road is that goes between the acres of potato fields. The county plows the road and if there has been sufficient snow the plowed snow leaves mounds on both sides of the road. Without a warning, the first few sleds hit that line of elevated mounds of snow and bodies and snowmobiles flew. Now, steps are taken by the support crew to park on the road so the riders can see where the road is located.

Some of the Warriors enjoy tinkering with their engines so that they perform beyond manufacturers' specifications. The potato field offers the opportunity for these mechanics with customized sleds to see the results of their work or in some cases, the lack of results.

"CHAINSAW" HOFFMAN KILLS A TREE

On one occasion, Dennis Hoffman, Roy Heisner's step-son, miscalculated a curve and ran over a small four-foot Christmas tree with his sled. Other Warriors saw his mistake, cut down the tree and put it up in the Grayling Holiday Inn lobby with a sign that read, "You killed my mother and father, now you got to take care of me!" Later that evening when "Chainsaw" went to bed, the tree was under the covers in his bed with popcorn all over it. At the Annual Wertz Warrior Banquet, Dennis was presented with a chainsaw to commemorate the experience, hence his nickname.

LARRY KING AND DR. WERTZ

There have been some interesting coincidences along the way. Larry King developed a very bad stomachache during the 2003 tour. Friends were sure it was something he ate or was probably due to too much brown bottle. Larry was sure something was wrong as he had never had a stomachache like this in his life. On Wednesday morning while the riders moved out for the ride, Larry was taken to the hospital in Grayling.

After an interview and careful review of X-rays, it was determined by the physician that Larry had an ulcer. Larry caught up with the group and joined the ride as if he only had a mosquito bite. When he got around to removing the plastic identification tag given to him at the hospital he noted that the doctor who treated him was Dr. T. Wertz. How is that for coincidence? Larry is on a Wertz Warrior Endurance Ride and in all of northern Michigan he sees one doctor and the doctor's name is Wertz. No relation, by the way. Vic and his wife didn't have any children.

JIM BEECHERL APPEARS ON "AMERICA'S FUNNIEST VIDEOS"

Jim performed quite a stunt on his machine and without intending to do so. While running a ditch line, Jim hit a driveway just a little too fast and hard, his sled launched and was airborne, but when it landed it bucked him off, much like a horse. He did a shoulder roll off the hood onto the ground and ended up standing straight up with his hands in the air ... as if he had planned it that way. Dave White got it all on video and submitted it to a television show, and by golly, the video was shown on national television.

LEROY CATE GOES INTO THE POOL

Leroy Cate's favorite stop was the Redwood Motor Lodge in Oscoda. They had an inside pool right off from the bar. Leroy wanted to go swimming but had no swimsuit. He was in the bar and was able to buy a use-once, paper suit. He dropped everything right in front of everyone, put on the paper suit, and jumped into the pool for a swim. Winnie says of Leroy, "He was a one-man party."

A saying is attributed to Leroy that, beyond his antics, may be his legacy. He would often say, "Nobody said it was going to be easy." To this day, when encountering a difficult situation, a Warrior may utter Leroy's favorite saying.

"HEY, WHERE IS MY LUGGAGE?"

At one time, a couple of police officers went along to help with safety. They helped with the luggage at a stop. They decided to put each rider's luggage in the bathtub with the curtain drawn as opposed to simply setting it inside the door of the assigned room. Nobody could find their luggage and no one thought to look in the bathtub. Needless to say, that was a practical joke that can only happen once.

WINNIE CARES FOR LEROY'S PUPPY

Along the way some extraneous participants have been involved with the ride. Late in the 1980s Winnie, Leroy Cate and other Warriors were at an auction in Houghton Lake attended by several hundred people. One of the items auctioned was a K.C. Registered Golden Lab — a little ball of fur. Leroy wanted the dog but didn't have enough money to pay for it. The final bid was $435.00 and Winnie not only loaned Leroy the money but ended up having to care for the dog. He had to feed it, sneak it in and out of the motel rooms at night and according to Winnie, "It peed everywhere!" Leroy did pay back Winnie and raised the dog. Leroy enjoyed a party, earned several "awards" from the State of Michigan, would like to party all night and Winnie admitted, "He was a fun person. He could get people in trouble without even trying."

YAMAHA PRIDE AWARD

One particular event remains a testament both to the fun and to the success of the Warriors; the 1992 Yamaha Pride Award. Any snowmobile club or organization in the United States or Canada could submit a story documenting what the club or organization did to help the community. The contest was sponsored by Yamaha. Larry Tomenello submitted an entry and subsequently learned that the Wertz Warriors had won the Pride Award.

Included in the award were a 1992 Yamaha Phazer and a trip for two to Nova Scotia, Canada to attend the 1992 Snowmobile Congress to accept the award. Tony Pype and Larry took the 4-day trip to Nova Scotia and attended the Congress which had representatives from all snowmobile manufacturers and all USA and Canadian Snowmobile Associations.

Larry reports that "It was really a great thing. The Wertz Warriors were the highlight of the Congress. We wore our jackets with pride and accepted the award which was a very nice plaque and certificate."

What happened to the snowmobile the Wertz Warriors won? You guessed it ... it was turned into a money-making activity. Tickets were printed and a raffle was held. The result was that many thousands of dollars were donated to Special Olympics.

SOME SAD EXPERIENCES

So far the tale of the Wertz Warriors has been of great fund-raising activities and stories. But there have been some sad, and in some instances frightening, experiences that have been a part of the Wertz Warriors story.

Of course any accident is sad as the desire of every rider and every event is to have an accident-free tour, but the combination of man, machine, and speed will result in some unfortunate happenings.

1. There has been one death on the ride. As a result of an accident due to poor visibility, Pat Modos lost his life in a multiple-sled accident.*

2. There has been one death in the motel when a support crew member (Bill Werderman) succumbed to a heart attack upon returning from Opening Ceremonies for the Winter Games.

3. Many injuries requiring hospitalization have happened and while the seriousness of this should not be diminished, the number of serious accidents compared to the number of miles driven by the Warriors is unbelievably low.

*The following appeared in the February 6, 2004 Traverse City Record Eagle. The headline was, "**WERTZ WARRIOR RIDER DIES IN CRASH: HE HAD RAISED $21,000 FOR SPECIAL OLYMPICS.**" The following excerpts are extracted from the article:

"Obviously we are very devastated," said Vic Battani, chairman of the Wertz Warriors. "We are a pretty tight group. They are like our brothers. We all have a common cause, a common goal, which is the Special Olympics." Battani said Modos's wife, Jodi Modos, told him to continue the ride, which included several more fund-raisers, because that was what her husband would have wanted. "He was doing something that he loved," said Jodi Modos. "He really enjoyed helping out the Special Olympics athletes."

Joe "Go Wings" Palmer wrote, "Pat Modos was my Wertz Warrior sponsor. We shared many of the same beliefs in life. We were like true brothers. We did many fund-raisers: pig roasts, turkey fries, auctions, polar bear dips, poker runs with all money going to benefit Michigan Special Olympics. After the tragic loss of my Wertz Warrior brother Pat, it was very difficult to continue the ride, as I know it was for the whole group. But knowing Pat is on my shoulder every step of the way sure helps. He is and will be truly missed. Forever a Wertz Warrior, Pat Modos."

Tony Pype pays tribute to Pat. "I met Pat in 1995 when he came to the ride through Chuck Zinner. I was chairman of the ride at the time. Just meeting Pat for the first time I knew we had two things in common: a beard and a mullet haircut. Even Uncle Al would say we looked like brothers.

One evening while in the Grayling Holiday Inn I was sitting with Pat. He thanked me for having him on the ride. He also went on about how proud he was to be a member of the Wertz Warriors and that he and his father are glad to be able to raise the money for Special Olympics Michigan. As we talked he said his girlfriend and sister were coming to meet him and he would like me to meet them. They showed up and Pat introduced me to his girlfriend Jodi and his sister Robyn. That year one of the stops was at Dingman's Bar. Pat and his family made us all feel very welcome. They had raised about $10,000 the first year. Pat was very proud to have his family and his girlfriend involved in their fund raising efforts. After the first year, Pat and his family went gangbusters in their fund-raising efforts, reaching over $20,000 a year.

Since the tragic accident that took Pat's life, his father Pat ("Pops"), his wife Jodi, and his family and many friends have kept Pat's legacy alive. They have continued to raise money to over $30,000 a year. Pat is missed by so many but his legacy lives on through Special Olympics Michigan and the Wertz Warriors."

WERTZ WARRIORS PHOTOS

Wertz Warriors Board of Directors

Standing (L to R): Larry Tomenello, Gary Kukuk, Howard Redd, Larry Ternes
Seated (L to R): Tim Kavanagh, Vic Battani (Chairman), Tony Pype

1. Bob Bradley (L)
2. Jack Morris (R) and Bill Freeham
3. Tony Pype
4. Dick DeLange (L) and Richard DeLange
5. Digger O'Dell
6. Bob Brockett

7. Sue Digiorgio, Administrative Coordinator

8. The 2005 ride was dedicated to Warrior Pat Modos.

9. Neil Foster signs autographs.

10. Larry Ternes (L) and Fred Duemling

11. Jeff Weber (L) and Pat Modos

12. Roy Heisner, 25 years as a Warrior.

13. Ken Baker

*14. The Wertz Warrior photographers:
Bob Sassanella (L) and Dave White.*

15. Al Green

16. Fred Duemling (L) and Ed Adams

*17. Vic Battani, Chairman of the
Wertz Warrior Board of Directors.*

18. Mark "The Bird" Fidrych

19. Loren "Winnie" Winsten

20. Special Olympics President and CEO, Lois Arnold with Larry Ternes (R) and Bob Sassanella.

21. (L to R): Jeff Weber, Larry Ternes, Bill McInnis, Larry King, Neil Foster, Fred Duemling, Ed Adams, and Roy Heisner

22. John Beecherl

23. Detroit Red Wings Great, Ted Lindsay (L) and Dave White

24. Tom May

25. *A group of Warriors enjoys a hot breakfast.*

26. *Pam Melby (L) and Rita Rosek*

27. *Carl Hart*

28. *Card games are common on the ride.*

29. *There is always a line when there's food to be eaten.*

30. *There is plenty of help in the kitchen when the Warriors come to town.*

31. Dr. David Mandy gives Larry King a pre-ride physical.

32. Pat Modos

33. One of the many presentations of money to the Warriors (this one from the American Legion).

34. Mary Lang, Secretary from 1995 to 2005.

35. Larry Tomenello and Digger O'Dell discuss routes.

36. Bill McInnis

*37. Sleds often need repairs. A semi carries
extra parts and tools for each rider.*

38. Rides begin before sunrise, or soon thereafter.

*39. Northern Michigan in winter provides beautiful
glimpses of nature on the trails.*

40. Wertz Warrior semis for hauling the snowmobiles.

*41. Randy Kuchenmeister (L) and Wayne
Reams play a prank on a rookie*

42. Riding trails

43. *Filling up the old way…*

44. *And filling up the new way.*

45. *Riding into town.*

46. *Sometimes the Warriors ride on no snow! The 2003 command center motorhome is in the background.*

47. *The Warriors are greeted in Houghton Lake with this ice sculpture.*

48. *Gary Vernier helps load a sled onto a semi.*

49. Gene Reetz with an athlete
50. Warriors and athletes pose for a picture.
51. Larry Tomenello with an athlete

52.

53.

52. *Snowmobile rides at the 2003 Winter Games*

53. *Larry Ternes and friend*

54. *Bob Myers with an athlete at Hawks.*

54.

CHAPTER 8

Joe Falls Chronicles the 1991 Ride

Joe Falls went with the Warriors in 1991. As in 1983, Joe wrote a series of articles about the ride. These are reprinted here with permission of The Detroit News.

In my 45 years as a sports writer, I have traveled with all kinds of teams — everything from baseball to football to basketball to hockey. I have never traveled with a team like the "Wertz Warriors."

These men — 50 drivers and nearly 30 in the support crew — showed me some things about life that were truly inspiring. Maybe it takes time to appreciate certain things but I saw more genuine love — genuine caring — in their 10th snowmobile ride across Michigan than I ever knew existed.

They knew what they were doing and, more important, why they were doing it. They were doing it for those who could not help themselves — those who got a bad break in life: our mentally impaired athletes of the Michigan Special Olympics.

I watched them closely — closer than they imagined. It didn't matter if they were old or young, rich or poor, they were completely dedicated to the job at hand. So they had little snow. So what? They went on and on because they knew what the results would be. They knew these afflicted people would benefit from their efforts.

They raised money, yes, but more than that they raised the spirits of nearly 1,000 Special Olympians at Sugar Loaf Mountain while helping more than 25,000 of our athletes across the state.

Maybe some of these handicapped people don't know what happened. Maybe they don't know why they are able to ski and skate and swim and run and throw. That's OK. The rest of us know, and we salute these men — and the two women, too, who made the trip — because what you have done you have done for the right reasons and you did it in the right way. You did it unselfishly. You did it because you care.

As. Dr. Roy Massin said when it was all over: "Joe, not a piece fell out in the entire week."

That's right doctor. Not a piece fell out.

> I am proud to be a "Wertz Warrior."
>
> — Joe Falls *(written following his second ride with the Warriors in 1991)*

Author's note: I talked with Joe Falls after he had retired from journalism. The more we talked about the Warriors, the more excited he became, repeating what he had written above. Joe was touched by these men and women and he was given the gift of being able to express his feelings with words. Thank you, Joe for your words written with humor and emotion. I envy your gift and thank you for words written from your mind via your heart and soul.

Sunday, February 3, 1991

SPECIAL RIDE IN THE SNOW

WERTZ WARRIORS: WEEK-LONG CHARITY SNOWMOBILE TREK BIGGER THAN EVER.

MT. CLEMENS — Ladies and gentlemen (and kids, too): If you'd like to have your hair done, may I suggest the Milana Hair Salon at 48542 Van Dyke in Shelby Township. They will do a nice job for you — make you right pretty — and besides, they will donate $1.00 per customer to the Wertz Warriors.

Yep, these crazies are back with us again … driving their snowmobiles all over the state — 23 stops and 900 miles — for the benefit of Michigan Special Olympics.

This is the 10th year they've done it and guess who's going the whole route with them this time? Flash Falls. No, he's not going to get on one of those animated lawn mowers — he will be sitting in the comfort of a van with all the ladies (and a few of the men) and he would be no place else in this first week of February.

I know of no finer group of people — none more caring, none more giving — than the Wertz Warriors. They are just people. Doctors. Lawyers. Salesmen. Cops. Shop owners. Truckers. Painters. Insurance agents. Landscapers. Auto dealers.

Altogether, there will be 50 drivers, plus 30 in the support crew — mostly fuel suppliers and mechanics. When they are done on Saturday evening in Mackinaw City, they hope to collect $270,000 to pay for the entire Winter Games, give money to every Special Olympics area in the state, and put some dough away in an endowment fund for the day when there may not be a team of Wertz Warriors.

In nine years, they have raised $1.53 million for the handicapped citizens of our state, so that they can have their special games. As you may know, Special Olympics gets no government aid, no special grants — every penny that is raised is raised by people such as the Wertz Warriors.

Each driver pays for the privilege of driving. Some kick in $2,000, some kick in $8,000. They come up with the dough out of their own pockets, plus a myriad of fund-raisers, everything from spaghetti dinners to dances to raffles to Super Bowl parties to carnivals to, yes, hair stylings. They put canisters everywhere in

Macomb County and ask people to help and darned if they don't help. They also collect money in their stops all along the route.

All in the name of one Victor Wertz, the old slugger of the Tigers.

Vic got this whole thing started in January of 1982. He was a successful beer distributor in Macomb County and wanted to give something back to his community. He chose Special Olympics as his charity. His idea was to do something different. He thought of rolling beer barrels from Mt. Clemens to Milwaukee, home of his beer company, but decided the distance and the winter weather would defeat them.

Vic decided to use the weather to his advantage and hatched the idea of driving snowmobiles all across the state. His original goal was $20,000.

They started with 35 sleds and raised $35,000. It was a wild adventure for them — macho men racing through the countryside on their screaming machines for … well, for what? Why were they doing such a thing? They were doing it because Vic Wertz asked them to do it.

The whole thing changed when they got to the Winter Games and saw these mentally impaired athletes trying to skate, ski and throw snow balls up to distances of 10 or 15 feet. You could hear the crack in their hearts as they drove into town and saw the courage of these handicapped people.

That quickly, they realized they were not driving for themselves, or even for Vic. They realized the need of those who were less fortunate than they were and that's where it all crystallized for them.

They raised $65,000 the second year, with 45 sleds taking part in the effort. Then suddenly, they lost their leader. Vic Wertz died unexpectedly in 1983 and nobody knew what to do. He was the heart of the whole venture.

Do they pack it in? Or do they honor his memory and make the snowmobile ride greater than ever? More drivers. More dances. More raffles. More spaghetti dinners. Pretty soon it became a year-round process and they raised $80,000, $135,000, $200,000, $235,000 ... until they realized Vic Wertz's dream of underwriting the entire Winter Olympics, for athletes from all over the state, by coming up with a record $265,000.

If you've ever tried to raise money for your church or your own charity, you understand what a tremendous thing they've accomplished.

We'll be giving you daily reports as they race through Skidway Lake and Mio and Cadillac and Fife Lake and Lewiston and Hillman and Alpena and Black Lake ... stirring up the citizens all across the state.

If you'd like to help them a little, you may send a donation to The Wertz Warriors, Michigan Special Olympics, P.O. Box 1132, Mt. Clemens, Mich. 48043.

If you happen to live in the snow country, keep your window shades raised and your ear plugs in ... because they may come roaring right through your back yard. They promise to repair any broken clothes lines.

See you Oscoda. Last one home is a rotten egg.

Monday, February 4, 1991

SNOWMOBILE ENDURANCE RIDE REVOLVES INTO QUITE AN EVENT

OSCODA, MICH. — Wait a minute. One day out with these Wertz Warriors and my head is spinning.

We made three stops Sunday, two in Skidway Lake and one in Sand Lake. Same thing at all three places. The town folk were waiting for us with open arms, ready to feed us and give us the money they had collected for Special Olympics.

But it was like going through a revolving door.

We would walk into the American Legion Hall or the Moose Lodge or even the Sand Lake Yacht Club, which isn't a Yacht Club at all but a bar that comprises about all there is to downtown Sand Lake, if you don't count the outdoor phone booth, and they would have all kinds of trinkets to sell us — tiny American flags, yellow ribbons, raffle tickets, dishes, caps, jackets, ashtrays … everything you could find at your favorite carnival midway.

Hey, they even passed the hat.

How could anyone resist? I even bought a button that said: "I am an SOB".

The little lady smiled and said: "That means, 'I am a Special Olympics Booster.'"

She also said there would be no yacht races on Sand Lake until they found somebody who could afford yachts in Sand Lake.

So, it was a dollar here, a dollar there — five bucks in a canister, another five in a milk bottle … three into the hat … about 20 bucks in all, and no sooner did we give them the money than they gave it back to us.

Congress might consider such an idea to balance the budget. Out of the left pocket and into the right pocket. They can afford it with all the raises they've been voting themselves.

But let me tell you something else: I thought I had seen Michigan until this first day of the Wertz Snowmobile Endurance Ride. The accent is on Endurance.

We left from Mt. Clemens at 7 a.m. — 14 vehicles carrying 50 sleds, 70 volunteers and one very tired sportswriter. Guess who stayed out until one o'clock in the morning, dancing at his niece's coming out party in downriver Detroit, and got up at 4:30, with just two hours' sleep? Guess who had two eyeballs cooked in their sockets for breakfast?

The wonderful part of it all was that my wife drove me from Clarkston to Mt. Clemens, nearly a 40 mile trip, for the start of this sojourn across the state.

When I woke up in what was the middle of the night, my wife said: "When you shower, turn it on only halfway because the water softener is working and the water may come out pink."

A pink body at 4:30 a.m.?

The guys are really going to love that.

We are traveling in a mobile home, Digger O'Dell at the controls. He's an old Selfridge Air National Guard man, and all I'll say about his driving is that he thinks he is still in the cockpit of a bi-wing Jenny, goggles down, scarf flying in the wind.

I keep looking around for the Red Baron.

They picked up $3,657 in the two stops at Skidway Lake. Skidway Lake is a neat little place in the woods, east of West Branch, a haven for hunters, fishermen, bowlers and bingo players.

The folks had two big signs in their American Legion Hall:

"Support Special Olympics."

"Support America."

They got no arguments on this crystal-clear Sunday morning. Everywhere you looked, there were gold ribbons fluttering in the breezes. All the sleds carried them on their antennae.

When we left, everyone was given a strip of stickers: "Support Our Troops." These now adorn every possible piece of clothing and equipment in the fleet. The main semi tractor trailer has a giant American flag strapped to the side of it.

They even started with a prayer hoping nobody will be hurt out on the trails or on the sands of the Persian Gulf.

Our second stop in Skidway Lake was Moose Lodge #440. They actually had a moose head hanging on a wall, and anyone who took a root beer out of the fridge put a dollar in the jar. The local legionnaires stayed up Saturday night making 250 pasties, gravy and coleslaw for the hungry drivers and mechanics.

From there it was on to Sand Lake, where they raised their money by throwing a dinner and auctioning off such mementos as an autographed baseball by Ernie Harwell, a couple of Red Wings jackets and a set of homemade golf clubs. The Warriors were given two checks, $4,371 from the people in Sand Lake, and $7,396 from a clay pigeon shoot at the Maybee Sportsman's Club in Monroe County.

The 50 drivers were getting fidgety and finally put their snowmobiles down in the mushy snow outside the Sand Lake Yacht Club.

They literally started on sand but once they found the woods, they began perking along.

How fast can they go?

How does 120 mph sound?

It should be an interesting week if they can stay away from the tree stumps and wire fences. This is not an easy ride, even for bleary-eyed sportswriters.

Tuesday, February 5, 1991

Mud can't besmirch Warriors' proud mission

HOUGHTON LAKE, MICH. — If this warm weather keeps up, the Wertz Warriors may have to give up their snowmobiles for surfboards, canoes or sand buggies.

The snow is melting faster than butter in a frying pan.

They are on course in their bid to raise more than a quarter of a million dollars for Michigan Special Olympics, but so far it has seemed more like a swim meet than a snowmobile ride. Or, maybe what they're into is mud wrestling.

Water, water, everywhere … .

They've been splashing through the north woods these past two days and sending up rooster tails large enough to qualify for the Gold Cup races on the Detroit River.

But guess what?

Not one word of complaint has been heard from any of the 50 drivers or the 20 people in the support crew. The mud is flying everywhere, and you have to remember there are no windshield wipers on these machines.

Kenny Baker, leader of the Warriors, said: "We look at it this way: If we don't have any windshield wipers, they can't hang any parking tickets on our sleds."

I seem to be the only one who has done any complaining. Our mobile home, donated by Jim Riehl of the Roseville Chrysler-Plymouth RV Center, is comfortable enough. My particular place happens to be in a cushy swivel chair — the coffee pot is nearby, and it is always available and the bed in the back is very soft.

But our fireplace went out Tuesday morning and the Jacuzzi stopped working and how much can one person be expected to endure, even if this is called "an endurance ride."

Especially since my idea of roughing it is slow room service.

Yet, we will carry on in the good name of Special Olympics, knowing that tomorrow's free lunch will be at Starvation Lake. That should be an interesting experience.

I mention Jim Riehl giving these people the use of a mobile home and if that sounds like a commercial plug, it is a commercial plug. He is just one more person who has come forward and tried to help those who can't help themselves, meaning the Special Olympians of Michigan.

Jim Riehl didn't ask for the plug, or even expect it. The Ford Motor Co. also donated the use of a 15-passenger van. Jerry Cook, of the Service Trucking Co. in Pontiac, came up with a massive tractor trailer and the people at U-Haul in Mt. Clemens gave all the hitches and a truck to carry the baggage.

This is what it takes to get this mission accomplished — good people doing good things.

We had lunch at Moose Lodge 1035 in Mio, and the ladies were ladling out hot vegetable soup and beef stew to the drivers and support crew. They even gave them a check for $1,873.17, no small feat when you consider these people are mostly retirees — almost all with fixed incomes.

And then, in the heart of downtown Luzerne, about 5 miles west of Mio, a man named Delton Jones came forth with perhaps the finest gesture of the day.

Downtown Luzerne consists of one intersection, and Delton Jones owns the Boron gas station on the southwest corner. The snowmobilers stopped across the street to fill up from their gas truck. But, lo, their gas nozzles were broken.

They went over to see Delton Jones and told him of their troubles.

He went into the back room and came out with two gas nozzles that normally cost $25 apiece.

"Try these," he said.

They asked how much would they cost.

He just waved them away.

I went over to see him later and asked: "Why would you just give them the nozzles?"

"Because they needed them," he said.

The name again is Delton Jones. His place is the Boron station in downtown Luzerne. Drop in for a fill-up and give him our thanks.

We stayed at the Redwood Motor Lodge in Oscoda on Sunday night. The rooms were listed at $50. When I went to pay my bill, the owner said it was all taken care of.

"It's on one bill," he said.

I asked him how much the room was, so I could keep track of my expenses and give the Wertz Warriors a check at the end of the week.

He said: "The rooms are 15 dollars apiece." Or just about enough to cover the towels, the linen, the electricity and the maid's salary.

Pam Melby, secretary-treasurer of the Warriors, explained this happens all along the route.

"People feed us, and the hotels charge us almost nothing for the rooms. They understand what we're trying to do and they all try to help."

Ten years ago, nobody ever heard of The Wertz Warriors. Twenty-five years ago, nobody ever heard of Special Olympics.

No longer are they put into buses and sent home after school while your kids and my kids were allowed to stay and take part in all of the sports programs. There are now training programs and competition for these afflicted athletes.

All this is made possible because of people like Delton Jones. Do drop in to see him and maybe even get an oil change.

Wednesday, February 6, 1991

Town's effort for Warriors virtually unanimous

GRAYLING — This is a story about the people in Lake City. Lake City is just northeast of Cadillac, in the woods on Lake Missaukee, on Route 66.

It is not a city as we know cities, but more of a town — maybe a village. I'm not sure.

It's not very big. That I'm very sure of.

This is a story about Tom Abel, Helen Nowlin, Bill and Sandee Baldwin, Ron Spangler, Skeeter Troon, Bill Mosher, the people who work at Foster's Market and the L.C. Fire Department.

I don't know any of these people and probably never will. We stopped by Lake City Tuesday, the eighth stop on our Vic Wertz Snowmobile Ride, and picked up a $2,100 check for the handicapped athletes of the Michigan Special Olympics.

They had homemade chicken soup and sandwiches for us. Plus all kinds of cookies and cakes.

We stopped at the Elks Lodge — the Fraternal Order of Elks — and maybe the people I mentioned were there and maybe they weren't; it was hard to keep in mind all their names.

But their minds and their hearts were there because all of them had a part in raising the $2,100 for our mentally impaired athletes.

They did it through an auction on the night of Feb. 6.

Here are some of the items that they and other townsfolk came up with:

Phil Foster donated an ice bucket. The Hair Nook offered a free haircut. The L.C. Fire Department came in with a firefighter's hat. Gloria's Apple brought in a Love Cake.

Then there was a duck picture from Holmes Ace Hardware, a cribbage board from Skeeter Troon, a one-year subscription to the Missaukee Sentinel and an outdoor thermometer from Foster's Market.

Tom Abel donated a saw, Arletta's, a flower arrangement, Elaine Sterns a microwave dish, Green Knoll one night's lodging and E.N.D. Service a case of oil.

And there was more.

Nancy Bowman offered an income tax consultation, L.C. Auto Parts and Hardware some bug killer, Mainstreet Cafe three pizzas and Kelly's a $15 gift certificate.

They all gave something, a little of themselves, a little of their town, and it could not have come at a better time … for this was the darkest day in the history of the Wertz Warriors.

For the first time in 10 years, they were unable to run their snowmobiles. They had to carry them from Houghton Lake to Harrison to Lake City to Grayling because the countryside had turned to mush with the warm weather that has come over our state this week.

These are rough-and-ready outdoorsmen, these Wertz Warriors. They like action. They like to be on the move. But again there was not one word of complaint … not one moan or groan from the 70-odd team … just some genuine thanks to these people all along the route who have come forward to help in this very worthy cause.

"Can you imagine what Vic Wertz would feel if he could see how these guys are handling themselves?" said Neil Foster, one of the longtime leaders of the Wertz Warriors. Wertz, the Tigers slugger, started this whole venture but died in 1983 after only two runs across the state.

Foster, 54, who owns a bar in Mt. Clemens, has been driving with the Wertz Warriors since the start, criss-crossing the state many times on his roaring machine so that the Special Olympians can take part in their own sports.

"My mother told me that if people remembered you one year after you were dead, you were a success in life," said Foster. "Vic's been dead for eight years and look at the effect he is still having on these guys. They're still running their sleds for him."

The oldest of the drivers — one of the 10 originals — is Roy Heisner, 66, another bar owner in Mt. Clemens. He is a mountain of a man with a backwoods beard and a smile that never quits.

"I will drive until I die," he said. "How lucky I am to be alive — how lucky we all are to get this opportunity to help somebody who needs help.

"I know we're just a lot of crazy people doing a crazy thing, but our goal is to take all those kids out of the back seat and put them into the front seat of life."

So, that's it for today, another day on the trail. A dull day. A dreary day. A quiet day.

But, geez, I forgot to tell you about the telephone poles in Mio. You should have seen them. Standing tall and straight. Reaching toward the sky. Strong, Powerful. Proud. Majestic.

Each with an American flag flying in the breeze.

Thursday, February 7, 1991

EVEN AN HONORARY WERTZ WARRIOR GETS THE ROYAL TREATMENT ON SPECIAL OLYMPICS DRIVE THROUGH STATE

CEDAR, MICH. — Mexico City, Munich, Montreal, Lake Placid, Sarajevo, Calgary … six Olympic games in all … and none match the opening ceremonies of the Michigan Special Olympic Winter Games.

Thank you, Wertz Warriors. Thank you, Vic Wertz.

It was another magnificent moment Wednesday night as the 50 Warriors drove down the side of Sugar Loaf Mountain on their snowmobiles while more than 900 handicapped athletes rent the night air with their squealing cheers. You surely must have heard them way back there in Macomb County, home of these mighty men.

Macomb County has every reason to be proud of the Warriors, for they give their time, money and effort to make certain these mentally impaired people of our state can feel good about themselves by taking part in the same sort of winter sports they see on television.

Ever since our government decided to bring the mentally impaired into the mainstream of life by moving the special education classes from the back of the schools to the front, the people — mostly youngsters — were able to see what life was all about.

When Special Olympics came along to tend to their bodies as well, the handicapped really came alive and began enjoying life in ways that were once deemed impossible.

Studies have shown that participation in sports has made them more educable, and when you see so many gathered in one place, enjoying themselves to the fullest, it makes you realize what a truly great country we live in.

Here in Michigan, the Wertz Warriors make so much possible.

They pay for these entire Winter Games, not only for the 913 athletes gathered here but for the 400 coaches and 430 volunteers.

They raise enough money to send a check to every area in the state, plus put some away in an endowment fund for the day when there may not be a team of Wertz Warriors to race across the state.

But it is more than the money that is so impressive. It is the determination in the faces of these men — the desire to do this thing, to raise this money, so the handicapped can live a better life.

You should have seen them loading the kids onto their sleds Wednesday and giving them a ride up the side of the mountain.

153

You should have seen these young people as they climbed onto the sleds, eyes sparkling, faces beaming, some screaming, all hugging tight to their driver.

I believe this to be the finest moment I have ever seen in sports … a moment where genuine love is dispensed with open hearts, minds and bodies. Nobody is getting famous here; just rich in ways that are marvelous to behold.

I'll tell you, it's great to be a Wertz Warrior.

They gave me a green jacket this time with "Wertz Warriors" inscribed on the back and this has stamped me as a very special person wherever we have gone in these past four days. People think I am one of them, which I am not. But that's OK because the treatment you get is so very real.

As I was walking through what little snow is left on these grounds, some of the Olympians, from Area 8 in Lansing, saw my green jacket and started screaming. They thought I was a Warrior.

"Sir! Sir!" a woman called out as I walked away. "Could you come back here. They want to touch you."

Touch me? Come on. Normally, you'd feel pretty stupid standing around letting people touch you, but this, of course, was different. I stood there while all the kids of Area 8 touched my green jacket and broke out in squeals of delight.

I walked a little farther and wound up in the middle of a snowball fight.

The moment the kids saw the green jacket, they stopped throwing their snowballs.

"Hey, that's a Wertz Warrior!" one of them cried out.

Another said: "We don't throw snowballs at Warriors."

Another said: "We love you, Mr. Warrior!"

Vic, I know you saw all this happen but I thought some of your friends might like to know about it.

You did good.

Friday, February 8, 1991

GIFTS, AWARDS AND AMENITIES WITH THE WERTZ WARRIORS

LEWISTON, MICH. — On the road with the Wertz Warriors:

They rolled into town on their sleds Thursday afternoon and were met with signs at their motel: "No snowmobiles."

No matter. These townfolk raised more than $15,000 for them — the largest gift for the Michigan Special Olympics on this week-long odyssey.

Most of the dough came from a summertime golf tournament run by driver Carl Hart and mechanic Tom May, both from Lewiston.

The presentations were made at the local Catholic church, where they served beer to the boys at dinner.

The pastor said they normally serve only wine on Sunday.

One Warrior told him: "If you ever get around to vodka, father, your congregation would grow."

When the fleet of sleds went through Mio, driver Neil Foster was given an envelope with $195. It came from the good citizens of Mio.

He put the envelope into his inside pocket … or so he thought. He missed. The envelope fell to the sidewalk and away they went without the money.

When they got to the next stop in Manton, there was an anonymous phone call for Foster telling him the money had been found and it was on the way back to him.

The Warriors have an award which is given to the person who goofs up the most in the previous 24-hour period.

Guess who is wearing the pin?

We wrote that the Warriors stopped at the Elk's Lodge in Lake City when it was the Eagles Lodge. An apology is in order and now the pin will be passed onto the unnamed driver who lost his Wertz Warrior jacket seven times.

"But I found it six times," he said.

The lunch at Starvation Lake was tasty. New England clam chowder, fish cakes, smoked fish and cole slaw.

All this was courtesy of the Hideaway Bar, which advertises:

"An awesome view of the lake; golfing tips; free manure; free matches; free information; weather forecasts; free parking; free fishing; free jokes; hot and cold running water; free bird zoo just outside the window, where you can watch them feed at the feeders at no increase in prices."

The drivers are wearing the following button: "Don't holler at me — I'm a volunteer."

The Donation of the Day came from a young man in Lewiston who collected pop cans worth $60.20.

He just beat out the local Sunoco gas station, which changed a flat on one of the support vans for free.

Some helium balloons were released at Starvation Lake with messages attached to them to send in contributions to the Michigan Special Olympics.

The record distance was a year ago, when a check came in from Wheeling, W. Va.

Casualty report: A dozen sleds have broken down and needed repair. All have rejoined the field.

No injuries yet, though Jimmy Beecherl hit a snow bank and went somersaulting out of his snowmobile. He is thinking of joining the U.S. Olympic diving team.

Once a Wertz Warrior, always a Wertz Warrior.

Tom Golds was one of the early drivers on this ride but moved away to Cincinnati because of business.

He has been back twice now to take part in this seven-day sojourn across the state and says: "I'll be back as long as I can drive."

Purely Personal: Until they put radios and heaters into these machines I am not interested.

Finally, a private word to Chuck Daly, his wife, Terry, and his daughter Cydney.

I know how you feel about losing Koko. My puppies are 13 years old and I hold them dear every day they are alive. I dread the day you have just experienced.

Koko was special and it was my privilege to know her. My wife and I hope there will be an Ame II and a Kash II in our lives. I don't know of any other way around it. Is there a chance for a Koko II?

Sunday, February 10, 1991

Wertz Warriors end a touching week

MACKINAW CITY — It was a week to remember.

They didn't have much snow, so it was tough for the Wertz Warriors to even think of putting their snowmobiles on the ground. They drove where they could, 10 miles here, 20 miles there — once for a whole 40 miles. They were supposed to go 900 miles but barely made 200.

It was sort of like going on a golfing vacation and sitting on the clubhouse porch and watching it rain all week long.

Very frustrating.

You can't take 78 outdoorsmen — 50 drivers and 28 in the support crew — and put them inside cars, vans, trucks and motor homes for the better part of a week and expect them to be very happy. How many lies can anyone tell anyway?

For seven days, they saw almost nothing but muddy roads, watery ditches and barren fields. It was more like April than February. The sun beat down on them from clear blue skies.

But they pressed on without a word of complaint, until the golden moment arrived for them on Saturday at exactly 3:01 p.m. That's when they came to the end of the trail. That's when everything became worthwhile.

They would get on their snowmobiles one last time and drive into town with a Special Olympian on each sled.

But wait a minute.

There was less snow here than at any stop along the way. Almost no snow at all, in fact.

"We're going in anyway," said Kenny Baker, leader of the Warriors. "We're not letting those kids down."

The dry roads — covered with dust and dirt, not to mention rocks and other debris thrown up off the shoulders — would have played havoc with the machines.

"We'll soap the machines," Baker said. "That'll make them slide."

When they got to the Ramada Inn, final stop in the seven-day journey, they saw two plow trucks pushing snow up in front of the hotel.

Not much snow … a narrow strip maybe a hundred yards long. All of it dirty.

"Let's go!" cried Baker, and out came 50 snowmobiles from the trailers and the trucks, onto the hard pavement next to a Big Boy restaurant.

And that's how it ended: a 100-yard ride with the drivers carrying in these handicapped people, some of them Special Olympians, with people cheering, flags waving, horns sounding … a display of dedication seldom seen in this often-impersonal life of ours.

These guys did it.

They reached their goal of $270,000 for the Michigan Special Olympics (actually $275,312.17), so the games for the mentally impaired citizens of our state can go on, bigger and better than ever.

This was the most money the Wertz Warriors ever collected since Vic Wertz, the late Tigers slugger, got this whole thing started in 1982. Their 10-year total is nearly $1.8 million, and this time they collected the money at a time when our economy has been slowed by the war and by the recession.

How did they do it?

They raised most of it before ever leaving Macomb County, home of most of the Warriors. They did it through their personal fund-raisers and from money out of their own pockets.

They topped it off by collecting money at all of the stops along the way, from Skidmore Lake to Starvation Lake to Black Lake — good people everywhere doing what they could to help these afflicted athletes of Michigan.

They topped it off in Hillman and went over to the elementary school, where the children gave them a check for $850 from collecting 8,500 pop and beer cans. They met on the front lawn of the school and hugged each other, the kids asking for the autographs of these men in their green and yellow jackets and these men throwing children up into the air.

It was on to Alpena, where Fred Duemling and Matt Giroux, two veterans of the ride, allowed their buddies to play "barber" and cut off all their hair to the tune of $1,300 in donations at the Elks Club.

At Hawks, the next stop, Andy Mauer, 25, walked into the tavern and said he wanted to give $50 to the Special Olympics because he was going into the Army on Monday.

On and on it went … literally nickels, dimes, quarters, and dollars tumbling in for the cause.

A week to remember, indeed. A week to be proud of.

CHAPTER 9

The 2003 Ride — A Diary

What follows is a brief account of the 2003 Endurance Ride in which I was able to participate. It helps to show the overall stamina required of the riders and support staff, but also to offer proof of the fun along the way, as well as the rewards that await the Wertz Warriors upon its completion.

The following is not a thorough accounting of the week's stops and experiences. The author apologizes to all who gave donations to the Wertz Warriors but are not listed here due to his being in the wrong place at the wrong time or not having the time to record each gift and who gave it. The intent is for the reader to appreciate that the people of Northern Michigan have big hearts and work very hard to support their heroes. The dedication of the people and their commitment to the Warriors can only be described in the millions of dollars raised over the past 25 years.

Each Warrior receives an itinerary for the week. The itinerary is full of details noting times of arrival and departure, the names of the route leaders, stops to receive money from fund-raisers, meals and lodging, and fuel stops. The itinerary looks much like what a professional athlete would receive on a road trip. For the most part, the times on the itinerary are adhered to. If the ride is to depart at 7:00 a.m., you can almost set your watch by it.

The hosts of the Warriors on their stops are aware of the arrival times and have food, drink, and people on hand to welcome them. At each stop, a short ceremony is held where a check or checks are given to the Warriors for money raised during the past year. The Chairman of the Board and/or the Honorary Chairman of the Ride, Mark Fidrych, will express their appreciation and present a plaque (s) to those who raised the money on their behalf.

After the Warriors have had time for a break, eaten a meal if that is on the itinerary, stretched their legs a bit, then it is onto the sleds or into support vehicles and off they go to the next stop to repeat the traditional protocol.

Sunday, January 26, 2003

The Warriors leave the Mt. Clemens area after having breakfast at Zacarro's, a tradition that dates back many years. The riders are not on snowmobiles. They are riding in a number of vehicles going up north to snow and a number of stops, the first of which is in Skidway Lake. The route leaders for the day are Howard Redd and Tony Pype.

AMERICAN LEGION HALL — SKIDWAY LAKE

The Warriors, semis, support vehicles and all 100 plus men and Mary, secretary of the organization, arrive at the American Legion Hall at Skidway Lake. There is excitement as the week is underway. The Warriors get food to eat, buy raffle tickets, and assemble for words from their leaders.

A long-standing tradition is begun when Roy Heisner, Dave Weber, Larry King, and Jeff Weber sit down to a euchre game. This will be repeated at every stop from now till the end of the ride a week from today. Roy keeps track of games won by the long-time friends. The shuffling, dealing, and playing of cards is accompanied with chatter, jokes, drinks, and good old one-upsmanship by all participants. When asked to explain what goes on while the game is being played, Larry King was quick with a response, "Roy normally cheats!"

Neil Foster, a charter member and one of a half dozen of the original riders asks for quiet and then introduces a number of people who come forth and present checks to the Warriors that represent money raised in the past year. Neil points out that this is the 20th year that the endurance event has begun at the American Legion Hall in Skidway Lake. Neil was instrumental in involving the Moose lodges in northern Michigan.

Several representatives of various community organizations proudly step up to the microphone to present checks to the Wertz

Warriors. Each presentation is responded to with hearty applause from the Warriors present.

Larry Boyce of Post 370 tells the Warriors that, "It is a great pleasure to kick this off for you again this year." He presents a check for $1350.00; Jackie Adamo, Auxiliary President gives $500.00; John Stetz from SAL gives $150.00; Harriet Church from LeFeemas 40-8 donates $100.00; the local Lions Club gives $100.00, and the local VFW donates $100.00.

Chairman Vic Battani makes some announcements, and with thanks to all the folks at the Skidway American Legion Hall, the entourage moves on to the Skidway Moose Lodge, for lunch. There is not sufficient snow to unload the sleds and ride. The semis, vans, and other vehicles move on.

SKIDWAY MOOSE LODGE

In anticipation of the ride commencing, the sleds are removed from the semis. Riders and support crew drive the sleds off the semis and they shoot down ramps onto the snow. Lunch is soon served and the Moose Lodge doesn't hold back on the amount of food ready to be eaten.

One of the long-time supporters of the Wertz Warriors in the area is Jerry Wester. He has a valuable collection of memorabilia from previous rides. He has an extensive photo collection as well as many pins and other items from Special Olympics games.

Gary Durkee, the Governor of the Skidway Moose Lodge, says of the Warriors, "We are always glad to see 'em here. The community helps them. They bring in money to the Lodge and we enjoy helping them. It's always a wonderful day to see them come in."

The sleds are moving and route leaders Howard Redd and Tony Pype lead the Warriors to Sand Lake.

Sand Lake Bar, Sand Lake, Michigan

The sleds arrive in Sand Lake mid-afternoon, and the Warriors are warmly greeted by friends and people who come out to see the Warriors. The people of the Sand Lake area have donated more than $200,000 since beginning their fund-raising, which by the way, began in 1983. Shirley Hazlewood, whose son, Mike, has ridden with the Warriors for the past couple of years, quickly runs down a list of activities that bring in money and this isn't all of them: auction, ice golf, turkey bowling, car show, motorcycle ride, 50-50 raffles. Warriors who have been instrumental in raising money in the Sand Lake area include Ralph Kieliszewski, Scott Bird, Gared Briggs, and Doug Koin, who, when the total amount raised from the Sand Lake area was announced, said, "Wow! A check for $29,000.00 is given to the Warriors — from a community that isn't even noted on the Michigan map!" The Warriors leave for Tawas on the shore of Lake Huron. The first day is history.

TAWAS HOLIDAY INN (OVERNIGHT)

This first night was dinner on your own. Super Bowl pools were created as most watched some or all of the Super Bowl won by Tampa Bay over Oakland.

Monday, January 27, 2003

The sleds cannot go down because there is not sufficient snow on the route. If they do put the sleds down, the route leaders will be Howard Redd and Tony Pype. Everyone gets into vans, cars, and support vehicles while the sleds are idle, stacked in three semis or in trailers. Next stop, breakfast in Glennie.

GLENNIE AND A VISIT TO DAN PEREYK'S LODGE

The Warriors stopped at a spot deep in the woods outside of Glennie to visit a friend of the Warriors, Dan Pereyk and his wife. A breakfast was provided in the Pereyk pole barn where the Warriors gathered for a short meeting. The decision was made to continue without putting the sleds down as the conditions didn't warrant riding.

The Warriors took tours of the Pereyk's home, filled with trophies from world-wide big game hunts. Before leaving, Dan presented the Warriors with a check for $2,500.00 for their efforts on behalf of Special Olympics, saying, "We appreciate you guys taking your time to help others."

MA DETTERS IN LUCERNE, MICHIGAN

While at this stop, I meet several riders and ask questions about how they raise money and what the ride means to them. Gene Reetz, Pat Modos, and Joe Palmer offer thoughts. Jason Mastropietro explains that he has a special understanding of disability. He is dyslexic and knows the struggles people with disabilities have. He said, "A lot of people have helped me. I can give back and this is my contribution." Jason adds, "It is unbelievable how happy the athletes are, especially when we come into town. It is unbelievable!"

I had the opportunity to talk with some visitors who were waiting for the Warriors to leave Ma Detters. Ann Plegue, sister of Warrior Wayne Schaldenbrand said, "Because we have a grandson in Special Olympics, we are grateful to all the Warriors for everything they put into this. They have given their heart and soul to Special Olympics."

Marie Clapp, who is Doug Clancy's mother-in-law and who usually comes out to support Doug and the Warriors, says, "I'm here for the athletes — to support their ongoing endeavor to be a part of society. This is a good activity with every penny raised doing a lot for Special Olympics Michigan."

The sleds go down (out of the semis and trailers) at Ma Detters for the first time and fortunately for the Warriors, stay down for the duration of the trip.

I rode with Mike Carden in one of the support vehicles. Mike was in his seventh year as a Warrior. He pointed out that no alcoholic beverages are allowed in any Special Olympics trailer/vehicle. The sleds are insured by the riders. If there is any breakdown in the sled, the rider has to pay for the repairs to the snowmobile.

I talked to a few Warriors. When asked why he rides, Chris Malik responded this way, "It's something I've got to do — give back. My brother had a heart condition and died at an early age, lived with it all his life. This is my first opportunity to give back. I thought it was something I could do."

Rob Bellia is the grandson of Ed Adams, one of the original Warriors. Rob credits Ed with his upbringing and introducing him to the outdoors. "My grandfather raised me and I never would have gotten into snowmobiling or hunting if not for him." Rob says of this mission, "It's a great cause — helps kids."

Dan Schroeder, a veteran rider explains his involvement this way, "The way I was raised, you help other people. If you are fortunate, have health and extra time, you help others."

ST. HELEN — AMERICAN LEGION HALL

The Warriors moved on to St. Helen where they met a huge crowd of loyal supporters. The American Legion Hall was packed to see the Warriors and to take pride in the donations that would be given to the cause. One of the women in the hall told me, "I think they (Warriors) are great. The whole organization is wonderful. One of the Special Olympics athletes is in my church and tells the congregation about the medals he wins."

Mona Lahar organized the St. Helen fund-raiser and presented a check for $5,631.10. She was thanked and given a plaque. At this time, a couple of the athletes were asked to approach the microphone and make some remarks. You could have heard a pin drop when the athletes were speaking and once finished, a standing ovation erupted, with the Warriors rising in sincere gratitude.

The day ends in Houghton Lake as the Warriors come into town. Before dinner many of the riders visit the "tool barn," the 4th semi, to get spare parts, replace oil, check and change belts, and put on new carbide rail bars. That evening the Warriors were taken to the Moose Lodge for dinner and a ceremony. There was quite a spread for all to enjoy.

Karol Sisson, wife of Bert, was on hand to present a check to the Warriors from the Houghton Lake Kiwanis Club. Karol says, "Our club saw this as a good way to reach a children's group on a different level."

Philip Spicer of Spicer's Boat City spoke of community. "What we do for the Wertz Warriors is a great way to give back to the community — we can motivate a lot of people to do good things. The community wants to support the Warriors. They are fun, enjoy camaraderie, work for a good cause and I'm glad that I can facilitate for them."

Before retiring, I talked with Ted May, son of Tom May. Ted is the paramedic on the ride. He positions himself in the middle of the riders and is equipped with a radio so he can be in touch with the command vehicle as well as communicate with Vic Battani, the chairman of the ride, who always is the last sled.

Ted carries basic first aid. In the command center vehicle is a backboard and a neck collar, if needed. There have been a number of minor accidents over the years and the addition of a fully trained and certified Emergency Medical Specialist is a great addition to the ride.

I also talked with Tom May who compared the ride to NASCAR, except the Warriors ride is not a race. "The machines are fast and the event is very orderly. Riders are generally positioned where they want to be. The riders are always fully focused on every foot of the trail because every surface, every bend is different. The machine kicks up snow and in some conditions it seems like going through fog. The rides look like NASCAR drivers or astronauts as they wear helmets, suits, boots, and gloves. Some of the helmets are wired for communication with the command center. There is a lot of precision in all aspects of the event: security, baggage handling, support crew, itinerary, meals, and times for departure are seriously followed."

Tuesday, January 28, 2003

The Warriors are on their sleds before sunup and on their way to Leota for breakfast and the first stop of the day. The route leaders today are Neil Foster, Chuck Zinner and Andre Ducoffre.

LEOTA — RIVERSIDE BAR

The Warriors arrive to an excellent breakfast of eggs, bacon, sausage, biscuits and gravy, French toast, and coffee. The Warriors had a team meeting where Warriors are asked to be sure and return tools and information is given about future stops on today's route.

It was here that Dave Weber got up and announced that Fred Duemling's streak of riding every mile since the first mile out of Vic's Distributorship in 1982 has ended. During the off season, Fred had had hip replacement surgery, but he had been cleared to participate and fully expected to have no trouble with the 2003 trip. But, after yesterday's ride, his hip was very painful and he made the decision not to go on. The record stands at 14,500 miles of continuous riding, never missing a mile in 21 years and one day. The announcement was emotional for all Warriors as well as Fred. Fred went to the next stop and rested, spending some time in a whirlpool bath and continued with the Warriors the next day as a member of the support crew.

Warrior Rick Thierry says of Fred Duemling, "A first class man. For him not to ride — that's an emotional thing right there. Every mile for 21 plus years, that record may never be broken."

I rode with Rick Thierry and John Walker in their security vehicle. They are the last vehicle and it is their job to make sure that everything is in front of them. "Every mile, every year is different," Rick says. "The road conditions, the weather — that's what makes it fun." Rick and John man one of two security vehicles. Digger O'Dell and Bill McInnis man the second. It is off to Lake City Town Pump for fuel and brunch.

LAKE CITY

The Warriors pull into Lake City and park their sleds across the street from the Town Pump. Hot soup was waiting inside and it was enjoyed by all. A check was presented and appreciated by the Warriors.

Billie Reid Daniels, mother of Pat Reid, the bar owner, said, "They said it (raising so much money) couldn't be done and they did it! It is amazing that a small bar could generate so many funds. When you get a group of people together with a purpose and a goal and they work hard to accomplish it — it is simply amazing what these men do."

Kelly Russell said, "I am impressed with the tenacity of the Wertz Warriors — 22 years of going strong!"

Mary Jackson, who is responsible for raising funds for Wertz Warriors, says, "Everybody is more than willing to donate time, money, merchandise and whatever they can do, they help."

Pat Reid praises the people in the Lake City area saying, "The Lake City community is so generous, it is amazing!"

As Hal Katterman was putting on his third set of carbides, I said, "You'd think with all the technology today and putting a man on the moon, they could make a runner that would hold up to various surfaces." Hal replied, "There probably is, but we probably couldn't afford it."

With full gas tanks, the riders forge on to Dingman's Bar.

Dingman's Bar (6-8 miles west of Kalkaska)

The Warriors are greeted by the family and friends of Warrior Pat Modos who was most proud to have the Warriors in his own backyard. Bar owner and father of Pat is Pat Sr. or "Pops" Modos. Pops was proud and thankful as he presented a check for $19,500.00 to the Warriors and said, "It's great to see a group of people that can still focus on ways to help their fellow man."

Are the rookies still having fun? "I'm having the time of my life!" says Eric McAlpine. "It is so amazing the community support up here. Here the giving is from the heart — a different attitude. Here they dig deep."

Mike Nowaczk adds, "I love it, man, and I think it is great! It feels good to be giving back to the community where we know it is doing good. If you can help somebody, somebody who doesn't expect it, and the athletes don't expect it, that is special!"

As the Warriors were preparing to leave, a school bus full of athletes went by on M-72. The driver honked the horn repeatedly as the Warriors and the athletes exchanged waves and smiles. They would meet again in a few hours when at 3:00 p.m. rides would be given to the athletes, the highlight of the afternoon.

I did not go on to Fife Lake but went to Grayling where we would spend the night.

Wednesday, January 29, 2003

Up bright and early in Grayling with a 7:15 departure heading to Mesick. The route leaders today are Jeff Weber, Gary Kukuk and Matt Giroux.

This is the day the Warriors have been waiting for. By afternoon they will be at the Winter Games and around 3:00 p.m. will be having the time of their lives giving snowmobile rides to the athletes. In darkness, the Warriors, being led by route leaders Jeff Weber, Gary Kukuk and Matt Giroux, pull out of the motel parking lot and head for a fuel stop and to Mesick Grade School.

The fuel stop is an amazing activity to see. These sleds line up at every pump and the support crew takes the hose and one after another fills the tank or allows the rider to fill his tank. As soon as the tank is full, the sled moves to a waiting area. In a matter of minutes, all sleds are fueled and ready to go! The bill is paid and they are off to Mesick Amvets Hall. A lunch is waiting for the Warriors who have arrived in quite a snowfall. Once again the rituals begin — card games, eating, receiving money, selling merchandise, and taking a well-deserved break.

At this time, I leave the ride and go to Traverse City where I have responsibilities as a Board Member of Special Olympics

Michigan. The Warriors ride on to Fife Lake and then on to Traverse City.

GRAND TRAVERSE RESORT — OPENING CEREMONIES FOR SPECIAL OLYMPICS WINTER GAMES

The Warriors look forward to the stop in Traverse City. Most see this as the reason for all of their efforts. Tom May, chief mechanic for the endurance ride, said, "A lot of effort goes into making sure all the sleds are functioning and that the riders get to Winter Games." Even the semi-drivers plan to have the trucks washed.

The Warriors arrive about 3:00 p.m. on Wednesday. A half hour later, athletes begin to appear for their annual ride on a snowmobile. Athletes line up and members of the support crew assist the athletes in getting on the snowmobiles. Arms and hands cling to the Warrior and off the sled goes, kicking up snow, with a wide smile and an occasional apprehensive facial expression on the faces of the athletes. The sleds go in a huge circle, over bumps with some straightaways where the throttle is opened for a fun and fast ride over the snow. Debbie Tate, wife of Warrior Fred Tate, says, "You know, I don't know who is smiling more, the Warriors or the athletes?"

The riders are dropped off with each giving the Warrior a hug or a handshake or minimally a broad smile which is all the Warrior wants. They then join their fellow athletes, coaches or chaperones and like being at the most popular ride at a carnival, many get in line for another ride.

Warrior Chris Malik walked up to me and said, "You asked me yesterday, why do we do this — this is it."

Quotes at the Snowmobile Ride at Grand Traverse Resort

"It's the best part of the whole ride."
— Brett Vollen, Wertz Warrior

"This is what it is all about, man. It makes my stomach curl — I get butterflies around these athletes. It's awesome."
— Steve Rizzo, Wertz Warrior

"It's really cool how they get the help!" — Lauren Laenen, teenage daughter of Wertz Warrior, Kim Laenen

"It was my first time (snowmobile ride) and I had a blast!"
— Marissa, athlete

"I had a great time! It was fast enough for me."
— Christopher, athlete

"It was so cool!" — Jacqueline, an athlete who got to ride on Matt's machine (her sister works for him)

"It was fun! It goes fast!" — Austin, athlete

"It was fun. I got to put my hands on the handlebars." — Lucas, athlete from Area 17

"It was a BOMB! [i.e. the best!]" — Steven, athlete

"It went so fast!" — Bryan, athlete

"A very rewarding experience for the athletes. They just love it!" — Denise Williams, coach from Area 18

"This is well worth missing three tests and a quiz!" — Hollie Gilmore, a junior at Central Michigan University, volunteering at Winter Games

"I think it is great that they fund-raise. What would we do without them?" — Barbara Smith, Area 23 – Wayne County

"It was awesome!" — Joel, Area 10 – Sanilac

"My driver was maniac Mike — it was cool!" — Mark, athlete

"He (Wertz Warrior) was nice because he went slow." — Alicia, athlete

"It was cool!" — Tyler, athlete

"Thrilling — going fast with the wind in your face is thrilling!" — Sami, athlete

"I'd love to be a Wertz Warrior — I love to snowmobile."
— Cathy, a coach from Area 10

"Two of the most thrilling events in Special Olympics is when the Wertz Warriors ride in on the sleds and when they march in during opening ceremonies." — Denise Walker, Coach from Area 10

Tony Pype adds to the emotions of most Warriors when he says, "I learned I had a soft side when we got to the Winter Games outside of Traverse City and had contact with the athletes. They were people, too. They like to have fun just like every other person, young and old. They laugh and had fun just like we did. The only difference I could see with the athletes is that they didn't seem to judge anything or anybody. That would also make them genuine with big hearts, the same as Vic Wertz. I learned that I had a great life and family and that the world was so big, it needed people helping people."

Joe Palmer relates an interesting observation and experience. "When you see the faces of these athletes before, during, and after a competition, you can never tell where they placed. The athletes have a tendency to give it their best and enjoy their accomplishment whether they come in first, second or last. My sister-in-law competed in the first Special Olympics Games. That was over twenty-five years ago and she still talks about how much fun she had.

"I remember my rookie year, after the Opening Ceremonies, I stayed afterwards to join in some games with the athletes. One event was four Warriors against eight athletes in a tug-of-war. They kicked our butts! I considered myself to be a pretty strong person, but they were stronger and determined to beat us. After it was over we noticed they had dug in the snow their biggest and heaviest athlete as an anchor. It was one of the funniest and smartest things I had seen the athletes do. I still laugh about that today. It always brings a smile to my face."

The David Mandy family has been involved with Special Olympics Michigan for years. As noted earlier in the book, Dr. Mandy gives the physicals for the riders. He and his wife Jane have three children and all have participated in the Special Olympics Michigan program.

When asked about the Warriors, Holly Mandy replied, "The Wertz Warriors are a big part of my Special Olympics life. Their efforts have allowed me to compete in all sorts of sports and have made some of my dreams come true. I enjoy riding the snowmobiles with them and they are always so happy to see me and the other athletes. They are part of my family of friends and without them, my world would be a lot smaller."

Joshua Mandy, age 25, adds, "The Wertz Warriors have made me feel good about myself by allowing me to compete in cross-country skiing which I love so very much, as well as poly-hockey and soccer. I appreciate all of the time they take in raising money for the athletes of Special Olympics. Without the Wertz Warriors, I would be unable to do the sports that I love."

Dr. Mandy says of their son, "Drew doesn't talk much but he LOOOOOOOOOVES the Warriors and their snow machines. Just try and stop him from getting on one of their snowmobiles!"

OPENING CEREMONIES — EARLY IN THE EVENING

Most Warriors will tell you it is the Opening Ceremonies that gives you chills and the sincere appreciation that is expressed by the athletes and all who are at the Winter Games. The Warriors gather in the area outside the convention ballroom. Inside, they are introduced, the doors open and the crowd goes wild with cheers, a standing ovation, and whistles, this expression of love goes on for several minutes as the Warriors come down the center aisle in their green jackets, smiling and acknowledging the crowd. The applause doesn't stop until every Warrior has reached the front of the room.

Rick Thierry says, "If you don't feel anything coming into Opening Ceremonies or standing in front of the crowd, you're dead. It changes you — you're not the same person. It is different every year — you get recharged."

After the applause dies down, Chairman of the Board, Vic Battani, greets the Warriors and thanks them for their warm welcome. He finishes his remarks and introduces Mark Fidrych and once again the crowd goes wild. Mark and Vic, along with members of the Wertz Warriors Board of Directors present to Lois Arnold of Special Olympics Michigan a cardboard check for hundreds of thousands of dollars which had been raised on the ride. Again, the crowd goes wild with cheers and applause.

While the Wertz Warriors Board is on stage, there is the presentation of the Vandersloot and Bunbary Awards to athletes who have distinguished themselves. They are given a green jacket with warm handshakes from the Warriors. It is indeed a special ceremony with much emotion.

At the end of the ceremony, Mark Fidrych pauses and says with much enthusiasm, "Let the games begin!" and the crowd once again goes wild with applause and enthusiastic shouts of joy.

Following the opening ceremonies, many of the Warriors remain in the area to greet athletes who have become their friends and to pose for pictures and to talk with those who wish to thank them or ask questions.

Ben Rizzo puts the athletes' participation in the games into perspective when he says, "It makes you think twice about what the world is about. It's a good reality check. It makes you feel proud to watch the athletes achieve their goals and enjoy winter sports."

The next morning comes too soon and the Warriors have left for their next stop and the sun has yet to rise.

This stop at the Winter Games is what the trip is all about. This is the crowning moment; this is special for the Warriors and the athletes.

Thursday, January 30, 2003

Under the cover of darkness, the machines are fired up. The air is cold and the heat from the sleds gives the impression one is walking along a London alley in a dense fog. The sleds leave on time, 7:00 a.m., under the leadership of route leaders Chuck Zinner and Carl Hart in the morning, and Wayne Reams in the afternoon. Plans to go to the Mancelona Moose Lodge and school are cancelled, so their destination is Alba.

ALBA — GREEN LANTERN BAR

The woman who leads the effort to raise money in Alba, a dot on the map north of Mancelona, is Jean LaPratt. "I love 'em (Warriors)! The whole community works together to support the

Wertz Warriors." Jean has been hard at work raising money for the past nine years. When asked why she does it, she replies, "We love the kids (athletes)." Alba raises more than $20,000 a year by holding raffles, auctions, and a pig roast. Note: Jean has passed away, but the community's desire to continue to raise funds for the Warriors remains high.

Morrey LaPratt, son of Jean, and on hand for the Warriors' visit added, "Every time I see the Warriors line up and come across the road, it brings tears to my eyes. I know it is something special."

Judy Reams says, "Brothers John and Dan Moore have been and continue to be very active in fund-raising. Without the force of the Moore brothers, many of the events at the Green Lantern would not have happened. John and Dan are dedicated to the cause!"

Also at the Green Lantern was Steve Spehar, guardian of a winter games athlete. Steve says, "The Warriors are awesome. It is incredible meeting with other parents and guardians at the games and the Warriors are there enjoying all the activity."

Waiting to welcome the Warriors was Pam Reisen of Selina, Ohio. She is a member of the Great Lakes Snow Dancers, a snowmobile club of about 15-20 who annually come up to this area of Michigan to snowmobile. Between stints of selling raffle tickets, Pam said about the Warriors, "They are the best bunch of guys I've ever met. They are lots of fun, crazy, and their hearts are as big as all the trails in Michigan!" Pam also said they always buy a video from Dave White to show to people back home in Ohio.

It was common to find a reporter from a local newspaper at a stop. Ashley Schlesinger of the *Antrim County News* was on hand to interview Warriors and to take photos. This was the first time the young reporter had encountered the Warriors. She said, "It seems like a GREAT activity and a GREAT cause. There are a lot of people in this place!"

ALBA SCHOOL

A special stop on the tour is the Alba Elementary School. The Warriors roar into the snow-covered parking lot and the children pour out of school seeking autographs and talking with the Warriors. The Warriors leave their sleds and give autographs to the children. One Warrior was signing a youngster's cap. The school children raise money for the Warriors every year.

"Every year we contribute money for their cause," says Kathy Larkin, Assistant Principal. "The children have a great time!"

All paused in the cold school yard as a short ceremony unfolded whereby the children presented approximately $100.00 which they had raised. Mark Fidrych thanked the children and school staff and presented them with a Wertz Warrior Commemorative Plaque.

The sleds were fired up and the tour continued through snow trails to the next stop.

ALBA SPORTSMEN'S CLUB

The Warriors converge upon the Club hungry and cold from a long and snowy ride. A delicious lunch of hot soup and a variety of items were set out for the Warriors. Those patrons of the bar not expecting a herd of riders and support crew were a bit overwhelmed at the sudden influx of men. The euchre game picked up once again. As has become the routine, a check for money is presented to the Warriors and an enthusiastic cheer echoes throughout the Club. The Warriors are genuinely thankful for every dollar that is donated to their cause.

Now it is time for the race, the only race in the week-long ride, the race in Tater Field. The Potato Field race has been a tradition with the Warriors. This is a time when the sleds line up, engines are revved up and with the signal to "go," the riders pull out all the stops and race along a white carpet to the finish line. Since there are no officials, no electronic eyes, no video cameras for replays, the winner is often a claim made by several riders. With sleds tested to the max and speed expressed in the roar of the engines, it is time to move on to Jake's Place in Boyne Falls.

Jake's Place — Boyne Falls

The Warriors arrived at Jake's Place in Boyne Falls. The bar, owned by Kim Rottermund, was wall-to-wall people. Fred and Debbie Tate have been, and continue to be, the force behind the fund-raising efforts in the Boyne area. They receive much help from the Rottermund's and bar manger Marcia McNitt. Fund-raising efforts began in 1988, and Fred proudly says that the area has raised almost $100,000. The third week in August is the week for Special Olympics fund-raising in the Boyne area. "In the Boyne area many civic organizations, private groups and many others come together to support the Warriors and Special Olympics," Fred says with pride. "It is remarkable how the people up north get behind and support the Warriors. By the way, Fred and Debbie are involved in many fund-raisers for Special Olympics. Some activities are in the Lambertville, Michigan, area and Fred even puts on a fund-raiser for Michigan Special Olympics in Ohio, at Ottawa River Yacht Club, a stone's throw south of Lambertville.

A check was presented to the Warriors and Mark Fidrych gave a commemorative plaque expressing appreciation on behalf of the Warriors organization.

Fred says of Jake's Place, "Over the years it has become an event of old friends making new friends that all meet for a common cause. A big social event of sorts that enables a greater reunion of athletes to come together for a greater goal of competition and comradeship. Seeing their efforts and achieving goals. That, for this rider, makes me very proud to be a part of the Wertz Warriors."

Debbie Tate also said that, while selling raffle tickets at the Flywheeler Convention last July in Boyne Falls, a lady asked her if she knew any Warriors? "Yes, my husband!" Debbie replied. The lady said "I would like to thank you. I am a coach from the Detroit area. The Warriors give the athletes a goal and a purpose which is so important to them and their parents."

The president of the Special Olympics Michigan Board of Directors, Robert Chapman, drove over from Traverse City to once again thank the Warriors for all they've done and continue to do for Special Olympics athletes.

Now, it is on for fuel and the ride over to Lewiston!

LEWISTON

Pete Petoskey, a community leader, was the master of ceremonies for the evening. Standing before a crowd in the St. Francis Church hall, Pete welcomed the Warriors and thanked all for their support. Following a delicious meal, Pete introduced Tom May and Carl Hart who led the evening program. The rookies gave their talks and fund-raising checks were presented.

The fund-raising leaders in the Lewiston area commented about their work and the cause. "I'm so glad to join with them in the Garland Charity Classic. Together we raised over $70,000 for Wertz Warriors, Habitat for Humanity, Hospice, Garland's Choice and scholarships for students to go to college," said Joanne Lesinski, President of Habitat for Humanity, Lewiston, Michigan.

Dorothy Shepherd added, "I've never seen a community pull together and give so much support to people in need. Lewiston is like one big, happy family. Citizens help out with their talents. If someone needs help, people turn out to help."

"There are just so many wonderful people who turn out for this event (Lewiston fund-raiser for the Wertz Warriors, held annually in the St. Francis Church hall). From what I've heard from the Warriors, our function raises more money per capita than any place they go," said Wendy Render, chairperson of the Wertz Warriors fund-raising committee. Wendy praised the members of her 2003 committee. Included were: Rosemary and Russ Pryor, Ruth Munger, Karen Brent, Fran Hart, and Dorothy Shepherd.

Vern Rhoades, administrator for Moose Lodge 2495 in Lewiston, noted that his lodge gave $1,500.00 to Wertz Warriors. He then predicted with great enthusiasm that eventually, his Moose Lodge would be the #1 donator to Wertz Warriors in Lewiston next year!

While in Lewiston, Neil Foster related the following true story to several Warriors who were sitting with the storyteller. "I remember this shy, young girl who was an athlete. She usually walked around with her head down. A few years later, when I saw her, her head was about half-way up, and then after a few more years her head was high. She came up to me and said, "You'll be proud of me — I got a job!! I work at McDonald's!"

Neil followed up this story with this thought, "That's what this program is all about, building self-esteem." Neil said he had a sister, born in the 1930s with retardation. "She had a good life but she didn't have the opportunities people have today, like Special Olympics.

Friday, January 31, 2003

The route leaders today are Carl Hart and Ted May in the morning and Wayne Reams and Larry Tomenello in the afternoon. The day is sunny and beautiful.

GARLAND COUNTRY CLUB

The Warriors and the support crew rode in darkness to the beautiful Garland Country Club, south of Lewiston, where a breakfast buffet awaited them. This setting was a stark contrast to many of the bars along the route. White tablecloths and plenty of room to sit and eat and converse was a switch.

While eating a delicious breakfast, the conversation turned to the great enjoyment the Warriors have of snowmobiling. The common phrase, "At least he was doing what he loved to do," sometimes is said of people who die while gardening, fishing, golfing, traveling or whatever their passion happens to be. Larry Ternes thought for a moment and said, "I'll tell you what you can do with me when my time is about up. Tie me onto my snowmobile, put duct tape over the throttle and send me over the Pictured Rocks up near Munising. What a way to go!" The people at the table had a good laugh, but each had to admit that if you had to go, Larry had a pretty good idea.

LOVELLS — RIVERSIDE TAVERN

The owners of the Riverside Tavern are Nancy and George Benjamin. At the time of the stop, Nancy and George had only owned the tavern for a few months, but their enthusiasm for the Warriors and their cause was high. Carl Hart had approached them about helping out by raising money for the Warriors.

The donation this year was $500.00 with the expectation to raise that significantly next year. Co-owner Nancy said, "We really appreciate the Wertz Warriors livening up the bar today!" Her husband George added, "It is a great morning when the Wertz Warriors come into your parking lot. They are a bunch of great people — this is thrilling to see."

It was outside of the Riverside Tavern where some rookie sleds were wrapped in saran wrap. When rookie Ryan Yakaboski saw his sled so "decorated," I said, "Can I have a quote from you?"

"Right now?" Ryan asked.

"Yeah," I replied.

"No!" Ryan said with a big smile. Later he added, "It's all fun and games!"

Rookie Warrior Scott Bird of Sand Lake, when he saw his decorated sled, smiled and said, "It's all in good fun. It's all good."

SWAMP II

This bar is called Swamp II because Swamp I was destroyed by a tornado. Pictures in the bar provide an account of the devastation. A full buffet lunch is provided for all in the Wertz Warrior group. Raffle tickets are sold and the card and dice games begin once again. Outside it is snowing quite heavily, providing a nice blanket for the riders when they resume their journey.

As in other bars, a check is presented to the Wertz Warriors and they are thanked with sustained applause and a plaque presented by Mark Fidrych.

LAKES OF THE NORTH

Lakes of the North is a residential community in northern Michigan with golf courses and a club house. Larry Tomenello has worked with them for many years in fund-raising endeavors. For the past nine years, support has been given by local and seasonal residents of the community. They have an annual Thanksgiving auction and raise about $8,000-$9,000 a year. Dorothy Francis, from Lakes of the North Real Estate, is the coordinator/organizer of the auction. Dorothy, along with The Friends of Lakes of the North, donates countless hours and dollars to the auction every year.

Another popular table game of some of the Warriors is LRC, a dice game of chance. Each player puts three dollar bills on the table. Each player rolls three dice or a number of dice equal to the number of dollars he has in front of him. The player must do with each dollar whatever the die indicate ("L" means give a dollar to the player on the left, "R" means give a dollar to the player on the right, "C" means to put a dollar into the pot in the center of the table. There are also black dots which, if they appear on the shaken die, require no action relative to a dollar). The players roll the dice and do as the die indicate until only one player has a dollar in front of him. That person takes the pot.

I decided to play at the Lakes of the North stop. Claiming beginner's luck, I won the first time I played. I played a second game and was among the last three players. Not wanting to take money two games in a row, I said, "What happens to me if I win the pot two times in a row?" One of the players said nonchalantly, "Not much. We tie you to a sled and drag you to the next stop." The other players burst out in laughter. I didn't win, by the way.

PETOSKEY (OVERNIGHT)

Some family members are beginning to arrive. Standing in the lobby of the hotel was like being at an airport watching people come through the gate. Family members stood in the lobby with anxious children waiting for Dad to finish whatever he needed to do to put the sled to bed, so to speak. Walking into the lobby, many Warriors were greeted with huge smiles and hugs.

The evening was free and many went to the Casino where a room was reserved for the Warriors with drink coupons and hors d'oeuvres. The Casino presented the Warriors with a check and they were thanked by honorary chairman Mark Fidrych. The last day will begin with departure at seven a.m. sharp.

Saturday, February 1, 2003 — The Final Day

The last day of the ride is upon us. The sleds are still down with the prediction that the route will be in good shape for the final stretches of the ride. The route leaders on this final day will be Larry Ternes and Wayne Reams.

Night Hawks Bar — Hawks, Michigan

When the Warriors arrived at Night Hawks Bar they heard of the explosion of the Challenger Shuttle by watching the huge screen TV. Some were glued to the screen learning as much as they could about the disaster. Others got the information and went about their lives thinking of the tragedy.

Patiently waiting in the bar was Sylvia Hartwick, her daughter Cindy, and a friend, Glenna McLennan. Sylvia said, "For this little town (Hawks), they do very well for the Warriors." Hawks has a bar, two stores and a post office. The barber only comes to town one day a week. Yet, the small community of 280 people managed to raise $11,600.00 at their auction. And, each year the amount of money raised in the auction goes up.

Glenda was asked for her opinion of the Warriors. She lit up and replied, "They are beautiful — a wonderful group of men. I'm so proud of them for what they do!" Warrior Bob Myers is proud too. He is the Warrior behind the fund-raising efforts in Hawks.

Cindy, a Special Olympics athlete, has two hats filled with pins given to her by the Wertz Warriors. When asked, "Do you love the Wertz Warriors?" Cindy said enthusiastically, "YES!!" followed with a huge and genuine smile.

The owner of the bar, Carl Altman, explained the history of the Wertz Warriors and the Night Hawks Bar. "The Warriors selected this site when they began the ride. Hawks was a stop to get gas and they stopped at the bar in 1984. Donations to the Warriors began to be recorded in 1986 and since then $100,000.00 has been raised in this tiny community. The community has embraced the efforts of the Wertz Warriors who work for such a visible cause. We know families with children who have special needs and that makes the effort in our community all the more important."

The Warriors headed west to the Pines Restaurant where they would have lunch and get fuel.

PINES RESTAURANT

Warrior Dean Cueny, is the owner of the Pines. He presented a check for $1,326.00 which was the result of efforts to sell raffle tickets, paper snowmobile sleds with names and the amount of the donation, plus some corporate sponsors.

Dean credits Esther White with his involvement with the Warriors. "If it wasn't for Esther White, I would not be here at all." Vic Wertz and her grandson Fred are in a photo. The first time Vic and company came into Mackinaw City, Fred was the athlete on his sled. In 1990, Esther asked Dean to support the Wertz Warriors and he started raising money.

On to Mackinaw City, the last several miles and the end is in sight.

ARRIVE IN MACKINAW CITY — HAMILTON INN

The final mile into Mackinaw City is special. The Warriors gather outside of town. Many athletes from the Mackinaw City area are on hand for a ride to the motel and the end of the endurance ride. Athletes are assisted in getting on the sleds and excitement is high. The Mackinaw City Police escort the Warriors into town. The Warriors and their passengers ride in single file along the side road to the motel where all are met with cheers, applause, smiles, and pats on the back, high fives, and shouts of joy. The ride is over. Families are united with the Warriors and the feeling of a completed mission is rampant.

I wanted to ride on a sled into town, the last two miles of the journey I had watched for seven days. Warrior Fred Tate had room on his sled. While I am sure he would much rather have given a ride to an athlete, he gladly invited me to be his passenger. As I rode into town, I simply couldn't imagine the stamina needed, let alone the courage, to drive these machines at high speed through miles and miles of trails. These men are awesome, absolutely awesome.

The evening of the final day, Saturday, is the Wertz Warriors party, put on by the Wertz Warriors for their riders, support crew, and family members. A spread is set for a king. Shrimp, pizza, salads, fruits and vegetables; a wide array of foods are available for all, as well as a full bar.

The bartenders for the evening have a story of their own. Warrior Bob Bradley asked Scott Jones to be responsible for tending the bar. For the past five years, Scott and his friends, Joe Koch (his right-hand man), Mark Reed, and Dan Fiori, come to Mackinaw City to serve the Warriors at the end of their successful ride.

Scott has come up from Florida the past four years just to do this work and pays all of his expenses to do so. His friends pay their own expenses as well. When asked why he makes this commitment, he says, "We believe in what they do and how they do it. It is absolutely beautiful. We take our hats off to them and honor them for all they do for people with disabilities." Scott has a nephew with a disability so he believes strongly in what the Warriors are doing to provide an opportunity for athletes to enjoy the Winter Games each year.

There is a program following the meal. Vic Battani, the chairman of the board, serves as the master of ceremonies. A few plaques are presented, the unofficial total of funds raised, a check to Special Olympics Michigan, and tallies of the ride are presented.

Chairman Battani said that $503,000.00 was raised. He presented a check to Tracy Davis, representing Special Olympics Executive Director Lois Arnold, for $285,000 to cover the cost of the winter games and he noted that $105,000 would be put into a fund that would go back to the Special Olympics areas for meeting some of their needs.

Tracy Davis graciously accepted the check and thanked the Wertz Warriors for their hard work and dedication to the athletes. Ed Dodak was introduced and also thanked the Warriors for their efforts in the past year. He reported that in 2002, 1103 athletes participated in the winter games and that this was by far the largest winter Special Olympics event in the United States.

As for the ride just completed, Tom May reported that 80 gallons of oil were used by 68 sleds: 35 of them being Arctic Cats; 15 Polaris; 14 Ski-Doos; and 4 Yamahas. The number of miles covered was 875. There were two crashes but no significant injuries. One rider had to return home with pneumonia and one was hospitalized for an ailment unrelated to the ride.

Mark Fidrych, in accepting a plaque for his leadership, acknowledged the wives of the Warriors who stayed home and also sacrificed during the week. He said that they were all "co-partners in the cause of helping the Olympians."

Tom May offered an emotional farewell saying that it was time to end his service to the Warriors. Tom said, "Once again we have met our goals — a ride without significant injury and with sufficient money raised to pay for the Winter Games. This has been a lot of fun for a lot of years, but it is time for me to step aside. Thanks, guys." While all Warriors hoped he would change his mind between now and the beginning of the 2004 ride, they gave him a standing ovation as he walked speechless from the banquet hall. *Note: Tom did return in 2004 and 2005 and will be on the anniversary ride in 2006.*

Sunday — Departure For Home

Everyone is basically on their own. Many of the Warriors are with family. A few are going to the Upper Peninsula to continue snowmobiling for a couple of weeks. Arrangements for all are made so that riders and support crew as well as all of the sleds arrive back in Macomb County or wherever destinations might be.

During the week, the entire organization made 30 stops to collect donated money, express appreciation with plaques, hugs, and handshakes, and rest for the next leg of the journey.

CHAPTER 10

"100 Men, 1 Purpose," — John Beecherl

While each man is a unique person in his own right, as all people are, there is a bond that exists when the Warrior dons the green jacket. Warrior Jim Simpson, a 10-year veteran rider, said it best. "You have a cross-section of economic means in this group that goes from millionaires to the modest income, yet for this week, it works. When we put on the green jacket, we're all the same, we're all working for the same cause." When asked why he joined the Wertz Warriors, Jim reflected the feeling of most when he said, "I joined them because I'm an avid snowmobiler and I want to support a good cause. It makes me proud, because if we didn't raise the money, the athletes wouldn't have the experiences they enjoy at the Winter Games."

Most men know someone who is a Warrior and as they learn what the purpose of the organization is, they wish to become a part of it. There have been and currently are several relatives on the ride, too numerous to mention. There are fathers and sons, nephews, brothers, and cousins.

The typical Warrior is on the ride to have a good time because he is passionate about riding a snowmobile fast and enjoying the endurance ride over a week's time, but if they get it, it being the purpose behind the ride, they soon realize that the effort is bigger than themselves. They realize as Mark Fidrych often tells others, the real story is the people who give their time and money to this great cause.

This was exemplified at the program/ceremony in St. Helen. As a representative of each charity came forward to present their check to Joe Baker, representing the Warriors that day, all Warriors gave a rousing ovation, expressing sincere appreciation for the efforts. When a couple of sponsored athletes came forward to give a short talk, the Warriors gave each athlete a prolonged standing ovation. This was a clear statement of what the week was all about. It was all about giving, all about love of others, all about appreciation for the efforts of people and not about the Wertz Warriors. Vic Wertz would have been very proud to see the Warriors on their feet applauding others as opposed to expecting or wanting people to be applauding them.

This giving to others was a theme all week long: giving plaques of appreciation, giving autographs to children at the Alba School, giving rides to the athletes at the Winter Games in Traverse City, giving handshakes and hugs to long-time supporters, giving to local charities as wallets came out and were opened to support raffles that raised money for their cause.

In addition, there is also internal giving to each other. A lot of teasing goes on, but one is reminded of the three musketeers and their motto, "One for all and all for one!" On many occasions you would see men helping others with repairs to sleds, sharing experiences, giving advice, sharing equipment. There was a camaraderie present that was a lesson for all of mankind which says in a way, "We're all in this thing together — let's help each other meet our common goal."

Here is one more example of Warriors supporting one another. Larry Ternes explains, "I remember Don Liposky, a person who would stand out in a crowd, but he had a way about him that with everyone he met, there was an instant friendship formed. We became friends on the 1987 ride but I never really knew his story … until now. As I was looking through old clippings of our previous years, I ran across an article about him with regard to his involvement with the Warriors … it seems Don has an older daughter, a former Special Olympian, and sadly, the same year he joined our group … his 17-year-old son was tragically killed in an automobile accident, and since he was a part of us, Don asked for all donations in his son's name to be given to the Special Olympics. I often think of him and wonder how life has been and now knowing this, I wish I would have made an effort to know him better. I hope to see him someday. Again, another Warrior blessing … because of this organization there have been friendships created and memories to be thought of … with each new day."

There is another side of the Warrior that is presented by charter member Larry Ternes. While he would do whatever he could to help a fellow Warrior he explained that, "What is special is the connection or a moment I have with an athlete. Every year this happens, this connection, and it is the connection that I look forward to each year."

It is often said that most experiences can't be explained and that the only way to have an understanding of something is to have the experience. It is hard to explain why the men do this work. Larry Ternes' father couldn't understand why Larry would take a week out of his life, raise thousands of dollars and ride all week for Special Olympics. His father went to Opening Ceremonies for the Winter Games one year and then said to Larry, "Son, now I know why you do it."

Larry notes that the typical athlete is so genuinely appreciative of the Warriors. They give hugs, want autographs, want photos taken with them and they cheer wildly when the Warriors come into the opening ceremonies. Bob Sassanella adds, "They want to give us something." There is that word 'give' again.

"It is when you come face-to-face with an Olympian that you become a different man, a softer person," Larry explains. "It humbles you."

Larry continues, "Through the years, many good people pass through our ranks, every one of them never expected to experience such a unique time in their lives. They have a rough idea what the Special Olympics represents which in itself is what most people understand about any charitable event, it's like a distant understanding. With many of us, it's up close and personal ... we actually get to know the people who are benefiting from what we do ... we see their faces, we can actually carry on a conversation with them, we create a human bond that seals our lives with each new year ... I for one keep looking for the same athletes from previous years because they actually remember!! What we do with them takes only a few minutes but that memory stays throughout the entire year. Sometimes I wish the world would look at life the way these Olympians do ... we are so intent on the idea of winning that we forget what really is important and that is, just to have a chance to take part in an endeavor. Seems fairly simple, but us 'ordinary' people tend to mess it up in one form or another!"

The Warrior respects leadership and knows that the goal can only be reached by following a leader, and there is a great deal of trust involved in each of the rides. This was exemplified in Glennie, Michigan, when Vic Battani, the leader, the decision-maker, spoke to the Warriors. He said basically that decisions to put the sleds down or not is often a difficult decision and one that he is willing to make in consultation with the route leaders. He told the Warriors that in making the decision he must consider the safety of the riders and the potential damage to the sleds. "Some of you like and agree with my decisions and some of you don't. But decisions have to be made and I make them and if you have any comments or questions, I want you to come to me, face-to-face and express yourself." There was a telling moment of silence before veteran Roy Heisner gave all of the Warriors a lesson when he said, "There are no questions. You are the leader. We follow you."

Several riders have roots to their passion and the roots are related to family members who have some type of disability. Carl Hart became involved because he had a sister with cerebral palsy and a brother who had surgery for a cleft palate. "This is something I can do to give back," Carl says.

Lu Ann Rheeder, wife of Warrior Rick Rheeder, explains, "About ten years ago I was involved in a snowmobile accident that left me paralyzed and thankfully I am doing wonderfully. I can imagine what people experience who have a disability for a life-time. I think it is wonderful that all of these guys ride so that the Special Olympics athletes can enjoy sports and competition."

Bill McInnis's granddaughter is an athlete at the Winter Games. His daughter, Lori Halt, describes a typical personality trait of Warrior members present in her father; "He never wants any recognition. He is here to help the kids and his granddaugh-ter. He is a very humble man and I'm very proud of him!"

'There are numerous instances when a Warrior will note that someone in their family has or has had an impairment of some kind and this adds extra meaning to this cause.

CHAPTER 11

Warrior Thoughts

Following the 2003 ride, a survey was sent to each Warrior asking them how they raise money, why they ride, their fondest memory, and what they would like the readers of this book to know. Here are their responses.

SURVEY QUESTION NUMBER ONE:

A BOOK HONORING THE WERTZ WARRIORS SHOULD INCLUDE THE FOLLOWING:

"That we riders really ARE ENDURANCE riders. We really do some hard riding." — Joe "Go Wings" Palmer

"How so few can do so much for so many. How did a handful of guys in 1982 who destroyed their snowmobiles on the first day, raise thousands of dollars and turn this into what it is today?" — Steve Peters

"Most of the guys spend their spare time year around raising money for Special Olympics." — Bob Carter

---

"Honor our founding members and those who have passed away." — Tim "Ted E. Bear" Kavanagh

---

"Offer a tribute to all of the businesses that have supported our efforts over the years." — Ron Cavallaro

---

"List all the members from day one, the amount of miles traveled and the amount of money raised." — Lou Campbell

---

"A tribute to Fred Duemling honoring all the miles he rode and what he's done for the Wertz Warriors and Special Olympics." — Tom Bolia

---

"Guys always will help one another out and that some of them are great mechanics. Also, the Bird (Mark Fidrych) is a great guy." — John Cahillane

---

"All of the things behind each rider that make it all possible: family, employer, friends, etc." — Kevin Lee

---

"The joy and the thrill of what we do to give the Special Olympians their day in the sun!" — Larry Tomenello

---

"Founder's vision, current and future goals, honesty of the fund-raising with thousands of hours of volunteers." — Mike Lynch

---

"A tribute to all of the people, from the Warriors to folks in Michigan, who make all of this possible." — Vic Battani

---

"Participants each year in the Special Olympics Games and the number of participants as Warriors." — Ian Schonsheck

---

"The gasoline tanker going into the ditch upside down. The celebrities each year: Mark "The Bird" Fidrych, Bill Freeham, Mickey Lolich, Jack Morris, and Joe Falls naming us the Wertz Warriors." — Fred Duemling

---

"The history of how it started (the original idea) and how it was carried on after Vic's untimely death." — Dave White

---

"The history, the changes through the years." — Ted May

"All volunteers, support crew/time and dedication." — Nick Perfili

---

"Meeting many people, working with other volunteers for our mission, and making new lifetime, true, friends that are 'real' people."
— Howard Redd

"Everyone is special, each in their own way. It's all good!"
— Scott D. Bird

"It's amazing that so many guys from so many different walks of life, with varied incomes, and different ages, can work together."
— W. Gene Reetz

"I suggest people assume nothing when it comes to the athletes. I was selling Wertz Warrior memorabilia at the Sugar Loaf Resort for the Winter Games in 1998. It was a particularly busy day and although I had help I was still swamped with athletes and their coaches buying merchandise. Now, you have to understand that the athletes who were buying merchandise come with varying levels of mental, and to a lesser extent, physical disabilities. Because of this, the vast majority have difficulty adding numbers and this of course comes into play when buying merchandise.

After serving several dozen athletes, one athlete and his coach came to me with an armful of clothing items the athlete wanted to buy. Each item was a different price. Some items were $2.00, $12.00, $15.00, $23.00 and so on. He had nearly every type of item we had to offer. When I asked him if he had enough money to buy all of the *merchandise he said he thought he did and his coach shrugged in a hesitant approval.*

As I separated the merchandise, I quoted the price for each item and began to write them down so I could add them up. I wasn't even going to try and add it in my head with so many items and the commotion going on around me. When I came to the last of the 11 items, stated the price and wrote it down, I began adding it up. However, before I could begin adding, the athlete said that the total was $137.00.

"Is that right?" I said. "Yep," the athlete replied. I looked at the coach and he just shrugged again with a peculiar grin on his face. "Well, let's see how close you are," I replied. As I added the last item the total came to … you guessed it: $137.00! After placing the merchandise in a couple of bags, I asked the coach if he had assisted the athlete in adding up the merchandise before buying. "Why no, I didn't … he added it himself. Besides, we didn't know how much the items were until you told us."

It was then that I realized that the price sign had been accidentally knocked down earlier that day and was placed out of sight in a box behind the counter! The old adage to "never assume" could never be truer!" — Tim Kavanagh

SURVEY QUESTION #2:

WHY DO YOU PARTICIPATE IN THE WERTZ WARRIORS?

"It's a win-win proposition. We raise a lot of money for a very worthwhile cause and help a lot of needy people. More than money, we give the athletes snowmobile rides, a pat on the back and a high five. They see us as "cool guys," not wimpy stuffed shirts. We know how to have fun and we help them to do the same. They related to us. For us, it's a blast. We get to ride along, hard and fast for a full week. This is probably what we'd be doing with our time anyway. We have some good camaraderie and do some serious snowmobile riding." — Bert Sisson

"I had been and still do work at the Summer and Winter Games for 16 years. My wife and I both work at these games. Our daughter is an athlete so it was from knowing how important this work is that I applied to be a Warrior." — Bob Carter

"I like to give back to society as much as I can. To see the athletes' faces makes all the work I put into it well worth it to me and my family." — Joe "Go Wings" Palmer

"... The KIDS. We take for granted the things we do each day; the Special Olympians can only strive to do only a few things once or

twice a year. All these kids want is to be held and loved and fit into our world. We are all placed on this earth to do something for someone. This is my chance." — Richard DeLange

---

"The fulfillment of knowing that our group does make a big difference for many others." — Howard Redd

---

"A great way to help others while at the same time enjoying sharing time with friends." — Doug Clancy

---

"I support the Warriors because I feel a need to help these fine athletes and encourage them to continue to strive to be the best at what they attempt to do." — John Beecherl

---

"Simply put: to help those less fortunate than I. While this sounds mighty noble, it really isn't. We all get caught up in our busy lives and easily forget that there are a lot of people out there whose lives are far more difficult than ours. This is my way of 'giving back' just a little to help make those less fortunate feel better in some way." — Tim "Ted E. Bear" Kavanagh

---

"I know a lot of the Wertz Warriors, I have helped in the past with fund-raisers and participated in them as well, but I joined after my

youngest son was born with Downs Syndrome. I wish I would have joined years ago." — Steve Peters

"Being up at the Games on Wednesday and seeing the faces of the athletes!" — Bob Bradley

"To benefit the kids participating in Special Olympics and their families." — Ron Cavallaro

"To help those athletes who need special help. Also, I enjoy snowmobiling and all the new friends I have met." — Hal Katterman

"To help individuals who have a little harder time getting through life." — Lou Campbell

"To help the Special Olympics athletes." — Douglas Koin

"That I am blessed with four healthy children and for that I am very fortunate." — John Cahillane

"My first opening ceremony. I was stunned to say the least. I now know what the Red Wings felt like when they held the Stanley Cup over their heads the night they won the championship. What a feeling!" — Kevin Lee

"Being able to help those less fortunate than myself; developing relationships with the caring people who help in fund-raising; and the ability to establish relationships with the Olympians themselves."
— Larry Tomenello

"To support a great cause and event and the chemistry of the group. To lend my service/experience as a paramedic if and when there is a need during the ride." — Ted May

---

"My son was in the Special Olympics program." — Ralph Kieliszewski

---

"With two healthy children I feel I'm giving back to the less fortunate with fund-raising and volunteering." — Mike Lynch

---

"Personally knowing Vic Wertz. Then seeing the great time the Olympians have made a spot in my heart." — Larry King

---

"Being involved with a group of dedicated people, doing what we are able to do for the handicapped keeps many of us coming back each year." — Bob Sassanella

---

"I'm hooked — the relationships I have made over the years represent some of my greatest memories." — Vic Battani

---

"I like to support the cause because the Special Olympians get a sense of purpose in their lives and physically challenge themselves." — Ian Schonsheck

---

"Help the less fortunate." — Wayne Schaldernbrand

"To help the less fortunate." — Brett Vollen

"To help out in this cause makes me feel complete — I love the kids (Olympians)." — Loren P. Winsten

---

"Caring for and helping the athletes participate in winter sports that they wouldn't otherwise be able to. To give back. Let's face it, it's fun to do good and raise money for a great cause." — Fred Duemling

---

"It's a special event for special people — the Special Olympians." — Dave White

---

"I donate one of the tractors that pulls the big snowmobile trailers, and the love of snowmobiles and Special Olympics." — Nick Perfili

---

"To be a part of such a well organized group of guys that take part in such a truly enduring ride to raise money for a special group of athletes who benefit in so many ways." — Scott D. Bird

---

"I thank God I have a healthy family and I wish to help those that are not as fortunate. I have a special fondness for sports and working with kids." — W. Gene Reetz

SURVEY QUESTION #3:

WHAT IS YOUR FONDEST MEMORY RIDING WITH THE WARRIORS?

"There are many fondest memories. Knowing what I'm doing it for — riding with the Wertz Warriors and giving rides to athletes. Meeting up with athletes at the Winter Games." — Bob Carter

"I have so many! First is my rookie year when we arrived in Mackinaw City and rode the athletes into town on the back of our snowmobiles. They put the heaviest athlete on the back of my snowmobile. My snowmobile was dragging the ground. Everyone had a smile on their face.

Another memory was when we rode the athletes on the golf course at the Grand Traverse Resort. When I got there this boy from the Detroit area would get in line and I would ride him around; then as soon as I dropped him off in the drop-off zone, he would run as fast as he

could to get back in line and get back on my snowmobile. I rode him around that day for the full 3 hours! Was too funny, and as we were riding he bumped my arm and the throttle pushed to accelerate. We hit one hill and launched into the second hill getting some serious air! Then as we hit the ground, he hit my arm again to launch us EVEN FASTER into the next hill. We got even more air! As I returned to the pickup area, a few Warriors laughed at how HIGH we got! Then as that day progressed, the athlete and his group called me 'Crazy Joe' and that name has stuck to me since. The athlete even won gold twice and silver medals. To really make me VERY HAPPY FOR ALL!"
— Crazy Joe "Go Wings" Palmer

"The first year I participated (1983), my fondest memory was watching Vic Wertz interacting with all the people along the way, how dedicated he was to funding the state Winter Games. Vic was a very special person himself!" — Dave White

---

"Going into a small town with fire engines and police leading us down Main Street with all traffic stopped (Gaylord 1984 from Lewiston, I think). A Vic Wertz driven ride in a blizzard to a spaghetti dinner — also driving my sled into the Little Manistee River was quite an event." — Fred Duemling

---

"I have many. Each year always brings new memories!" — Winnie Winsten

---

"My first year on the ride, at Grand Traverse for the Opening Ceremonies." — Brett Vollen

---

"The first year coming to Sugar Loaf Mountain." — Wayne Schaldenbrand

---

"The Opening Ceremony is the most moving. Giving snowmobile rides is also great!" — Ian Schonsheck

---

"Wow — very difficult to answer. Every year creates a fond memory. But the one that stands out was my first Opening Ceremonies and the first Indoor Opening Ceremonies." — Vic Battani

---

"One of my first years (at Sugar Loaf), I watched a tug-of-war between athletes and college volunteers. Of course, the athletes won. First in line for the winners was a young man. When victory was won, this youngster with a big smile on his face leaped straight up in the air (looked like about 3 feet). That smile and leap has always stuck with me." — Bob Sassanella

---

"The year Eunice Kennedy arrived for Opening Ceremonies at Sugar Loaf Ski Resort. It was below zero." — Larry King

---

"Giving the athletes rides in Traverse City; giving an athlete a ride to the finish line in Mackinaw City; marching into the Opening Ceremonies like a hero; seeing how generous the little towns can be; and meeting all the volunteers and other Warriors." — W. Gene Reetz

---

"The Opening Ceremonies on the first year I was on the ride." —Ralph Kieliszewski

---

"Entering Grand Traverse Convention Center and seeing 1,000 plus cheer us on like celebrities." — Mike Lynch

---

"My first year on the ride and Opening Ceremonies and the ski hill — the cheer of the athletes and response of the crowd toward the Wertz Warriors. It was then that I really knew what it was all about and that I wanted to be a part of it for a long time." — Ted May

---

"Attending my first winter game competition in 1991. The interaction with the Olympians and coaches. I realized I would be a part of this family from that day forward." — Larry Tomenello

---

"My father loved kids and after he died I promised him that I would do something special for him. Because he loved kids so, I thought this would be a perfect thing for me to do. My first year on the ride (2000), they told me if you shed a tear while giving the athletes a ride to pull

your face mask down over your face so the athletes do not see you cry. I thought I could never get upset giving the athletes a ride on my snowmobile. Boy was I wrong, the first athlete I gave a ride to, was the same age as my father, and looked just like him. I could not get my face mask down fast enough. I will never forget that day." — Kevin Lee

---

"In 2002 we didn't ride but two days, so I really didn't feel I was totally accepted. I was also not sure of my riding skills. Riding with Pat Modos, Joe Palmer, Rob Mellia, and Dan Schroeder and Gene Reefs taught me a lot more about riding and by the last day I finally felt I belonged." — John Cahillane

---

"The grand opening of the Winter Olympics and riding with all the Wertz Warriors." — Douglas Koin

---

"I really don't have one. The entire 10 years is a fond memory." — Lou Campbell

---

"My first year when the Special Olympians saw my green jacket, came up to me, hugged me and asked for my signature, and told me about the events they were in. Some even remember me year after year." — Tom Bolia

---

"The grand Opening Ceremonies my rookie year." — Hal Katterman

---

"Pay day Wednesday, at Winter Games. Some people think we do this for 'free,' they are all wrong, we get paid big time on Wednesday at 3:00 p.m. when the athletes take US for a ride and at the 7:00 p.m. Opening Ceremonies. The excitement and joy you see in the athletes is indescribable and worth all of the effort put forth by all of us."
— Steve Peters

"Every year when we gather to give the kids of Special Olympics rides on our snow machines. The highlight of our ride is to see their faces light up with excitement as each child gets their turn on a snowmobile." — Ron Cavallaro

---

"Seeing the athletes for the first time. To see how hard they work and how happy they are to be there." — John Beecherl

---

"How overwhelming the Opening Ceremony is every year. It is a real highlight of the week, also reminds me of how fortunate I am to have such a wonderful family at home." — Doug Clancy

---

"Each and every Opening Ceremony and riding with the kids. It is great to be with the Warriors every year; there are so many fond memories." — Richard DeLange

---

"The fondest memory is walking into the auditorium at Traverse City and seeing all the athletes. I remember Mark Fidrych saying how much power was in that room!" — Nick Perfili

---

"I will call my fondest memory 'The Green Jacket.' It was 1997 and the guy who was to help me sell memorabilia suddenly told me only days before the trip that he couldn't go on the ride. Too late to find another assistant, I was left entirely by myself and I was really apprehensive about the trip. Of particular concern to me was the fact that on the 3rd day of the trip I had to leave the group and go alone to Sugar Loaf Mountain where the Opening Ceremonies and games were to be held that week. Literally thousands of people would be there — including over 900 athletes.

"You see, I would be the FIRST Wertz Warrior to appear at the games and I wasn't at all sure what to expect. I have been told by several veteran Wertz Warriors that being the first 'green jacket' at the games is a tremendous 'privilege and honor.' I would be, 'Treated like a king,' they said. I would also be 'surrounded by arriving athletes requesting my autograph,' they would say. 'You will be looked upon as a hero by not only the athletes but by the SOM staff as well!'

"After hearing these things I thought that surely this was a 'put-on' only to assuage my fears after being left a one-man show on the road for the first time. In any event I did what had to be done, even if I was by myself.

"As I arrived at Sugar Loaf, I approached the first 'check-point' that was staffed (quite unexpectedly) by the National Guard Reservist dressed in fatigues. No one bothered to mention to me that the National Guard was involved in this event! Good grief, I thought! I have no special credentials, no pass, no nothing! They'll never let me in, I thought.

"I cautiously approached the Guard, who by the way, had to stand 6 foot 5 with a square jaw and a 'no-nonsense' look. As I rolled down my window to explain why I was there in a big truck with no credentials, he said, 'Oh, yes, sir, you're with the Wertz Warriors...' and dutifully pointed to where I needed to park to check in!

"When I arrived at the front of the building, I was greeted by another National Guard member. He too explained — without my even asking — where I needed to be to check in.

"Now comes the real moment of 'discovery': as I walked into the lobby which by now was abuzz with athletes and their coaches getting checked in, it became eerily quiet. Fearing that I had walked into some sort of ceremony, I stopped and looked around to see why everyone had become so silent. Before I could comprehend what was happening, I heard someone shout, 'The Warriors are here! The Warriors are here!' I was then immediately surrounded by no less than a half-dozen athletes and their coaches. Each athlete had a pen, pencil, crayon or any other writing device they could get their hands on and asked that I give them my autograph!

"When the first athlete asked me for my autograph, he shoved a pen in my hand but had no paper or anything else to write on. When I asked what he wanted me to autograph, he said, 'Why, my arm!' 'Your arm?' I asked. 'You really don't want me to sign your arm, do you?' Before he could answer, his coach said that it really was okay to sign his arm.

"I carefully signed his arm, 'Tim Kavanagh, Rider #402.' After nearly a half-hour and a dozen autographs later, I finally made it to the front desk which was only about 50 feet away. Once there, I was greeted by Special Olympics Michigan staff and immediately invited to a special VIP banquet to be held later that evening.

"When I arrived at the banquet, I was seated at a special table and surrounded by Special Olympics Michigan staff that saw to my every need. It truly was one of the warmest welcomes I had ever experienced among perfect strangers.

"It wasn't until I was leaving two days later as I joined up with the rest of the Warriors after Opening Ceremonies the previous night, that I experienced an epiphany. While walking out of the building after checking out, I happened to run into the Special Olympian who was the recipient of my very first autograph. I remember his saying 'Warriors rock' as I walked by while at the same time giving me a high five. As he did so I couldn't help but notice my autograph on his arm just as clear as when I wrote it two days earlier. I clearly was a hero after all." — Tim Kavanagh

"The sincere joy that we bring to the athletes when they get to go on the snowmobile rides in Traverse City. And that there is truly a feeling that with the whole organization, everyone matters." —Scott D. Bird

---

"My first year on Wednesday just after opening ceremonies, a group of "rookies" (including myself) met with some parents of the athletes. This reception for parents and families with a few of us Warriors made me understand what giving so little and getting so much in return can do." — Howard Redd

---

CHAPTER 12

Index of Nicknames

Most of the Warriors have a nickname. Some were the result of experiences associated with the ride, and some were long-standing. Below is a partial list of the nicknames of many Warriors and a bit of the background that reveals the sense of camaraderie and fun that have kept the ride going for 25 years, and will ensure that it continues in the future. This is also a monument to former and current participants who have made the ride what it is today.

VIC "SKIPPY" BATTANI: *In 1983 at the North Channel Yacht Club, Vic's mom was playing cards and referred to her son as "Skip." Ken Baker heard it, perked his ears up and from that time on, Vic has been "Skippy."*

HOWARD "THE DUCK" REDD: *During the 1984 or '85 endurance ride it was a warm day and there was no snow left, many were riding on mud. Ken Baker referred to Howard as the duck and it stuck.*

DENNIS "CHAINSAW" HOFFMAN: *Dennis took down a couple of trees with his snowmobile and the nickname became obvious.*

ROB "SERGEI" BELLIA: *Rob bears a strong resemblance to Sergei Fedorov of the Detroit Red Wings.*

WAYNE "HERSHEL" REAMS: *Wayne couldn't remember names and called these unknowns, Hershel. He too became "Hershel."*

BOB "CRAZY" MYERS: *The nickname relates to his motorcycle riding.*

ROY "SIR ROY" HEISNER: *Roy owned a bar named "Sir Roy."*

DOUG "BIG DUMB" SCHOFIELD: *According to some, the nickname is self-explanatory.*

ROY "LITTLE DUMB" KING: *Roy is the son of King Dumb and has done some rowdy and dumb things.*

LARRY "KING DUMB" KING: *Larry is the father of Little Dumb and like son like father, has done some rowdy and dumb things.*

FRED "SPLASH" DUEMLING: *Fred drove his snowmobile into the Little Manistee River and the nickname was quick to follow.*

BILL "THIS SIDE UP" MCINNIS: *On a cold and snowy day coming out of Traverse City a car stopped suddenly in front of the fuel truck to make a left turn. In order to avoid a collision, Marv Claeys veered to the right off the highway down a slight slope and the fuel truck turned over on its side. No one was hurt, only some pride. Therefore the name, "This side up."*

DONALD "DIGGER" O'DELL: *This nickname came from an old radio show, "Digger O'Dell."*

RICK "TOBY" THIERRY AND JOHN "BUCKWHEAT" WALKER: *Giving directions via radio in the command vehicle, John Beecherl needed uncommon names for his men. He used John's nickname of many years, "Buckwheat," and John and Rick agreed on "Toby."*

MIKE "CRASH" MALIK: *Mike ran into Ken Baker's sled on Lake St. Clair during a pre-run publicity event with* The Macomb Daily. *A helicopter with a photographer on board swooped down for a photo and ...*

WAYNE "TOOL BOX" SCHALDENBRAND: *Wayne carried a whole bunch of extra tools and parts for fixing his snowmobile.*

JIM "POTATO" CRYSAK AND AL "TOMATO" MCHENRY: *Jim and Al were potato and tomato farmers, respectively; Jim, in the Bay City area, and Al, in Monroe.*

JASON "THOR" MASTROPIETRO: *Jason wore a metal jacket protector.*

NEIL "BREEZE" FOSTER: *Neil was known for talking all the time.*

KEN "BUBBA" BAKER: *Ken was chairman for several years and was the original big and burly guy with a deep voice.*

JOHN "IMAGE" MCMULLEN OR "JOHNNY MAC FROM PONTIAC:" *John would get up in front of the group if they were loud and a bit unruly and he would say that the Warriors needed to be concerned with their image. He was a man who owned a Cadillac dealership and everybody liked him and listened to him. He was a leader.*

DICK "BRUFF" DELANGE: *Dick was in charge of the support crew for a few years. He was sort of a drill sergeant and often wore a military helmet.*

Bob "Roll Over" Bradley: *Bob rolled his sled down Sugar Loaf Mountain.*

Ned "Trust Me" Cavallaro: *Ned would often say, "Trust me" when he wasn't sure the way to go, "Trust me" and more times than not, the riders would end up taking the long way to their destination.*

Jeff "Goober" Weber: *One year Jeff was up north with another Warrior marking trails and was acting up a bit in a bar. The waitress came up to him and said, "What's your problem, Goober?" The name stuck.*

Bob "Chief" Boyle: *At one time the staff at Selfridge Air Base sponsored Bob's ride and the staff decorated his sled — camouflaged it really.*

Al "Uncle Al" Green: *Everyone just called Al "Uncle Al."*

Bill "Wild Bill" Werderman: *His band was called "The Unholy Beast." He was a wild type guy.*

Ed "Round-the- Block" Adams: *Ed was the route leader, got lost, and took the Warriors around in circles.*

LARRY "TURN AROUND" TERNES: *On one occasion, as Route Leader, Larry kept going in circles for 15-20 minutes.*

CHARLIE "TUNA" PEYERK: *This nickname comes from the Charlie the Tuna television commercial.*

DR. "TOOTH FAIRY" BATUK: *He was a dentist.*

TIM "TED E. BEAR" KAVANAGH: *While on his first ride, he was repeatedly called "Ted" instead of "Tim" by a Special Olympics representative. When he was introduced to an athlete, he was introduced as "Ted E. Bear" and the name stuck.*

IN MEMORIAM:

Marv Claeys

Neil Foster

Earl McGregor

Allan McHenry

Pat Modos

Vince Nasso

Eddie Palenkas, Sr.

Rod Szalkowski

Bill Verdi

Vic Wertz

Bill Werderman

CHAPTER 13

Memorial for Wertz Warriors

Probably the greatest tribute a Warrior can receive is to have lived a life of service to his fellow man. Since 1982, ten men have passed away. Each man gave his gift to children and adults with disabilities by participating in a very unique event to see that people less fortunate than they had opportunities they would not have had had it not been for the collective work of many to raise money for the Special Olympics Winter Games.

The Wertz Warriors Organization and Special Olympics Michigan hereby honor those men who have passed on. May their souls rest in peace and may we the living remember their unselfish giving and love of others while with us on earth.

CHAPTER 14

Wertz Warriors

Below can be found the list of Wertz Warriors from 1982-2005. The list does not differentiate between rider and support crew as each person is a Warrior. Thanks to Sue DiGiorgio of the Wertz Warrior office for providing records.

1982 — THE INAUGURAL RIDE

The following participated in the first ride as riders or support persons. There were 31 riders and 14 support persons.

Ed Adams	Fred Duemling	Dave Jackson
Ken Baker	Murray Finkbeiner	Mike Jackson
Carlo Barone	Neil Foster	Tom Jackson
Marv Claeys	Tom Franz	Larry King
Mitch Cohoon	Tom Golds	Joe Klinghammer
Rick Demerse	Don Gooley	Kent Kukuk
Rick Drinkhorn	Roy Heisner	Tony Kulka

Jim Lamb	Leo Niedzwecki	Vito Strolis
Tracy Leslie	Jim Olender	Larry Ternes
Jerry McCaffrey	Ed Palenkas, Sr.	Howard Trombly
Bill McInnis	Tom Pardon	John Van Camp
Robert Marcereau	Roger Pype	Jeff Weber
Pam Melby	Dan Schmuck	Vic Wertz
John Molso	Larry Spencer	Dave Yonka
Jack Moore, Jr.	Paul Stoltman	

ALL-TIME WERTZ WARRIORS

The numbers in parentheses are the number of years the Warrior went on the ride. Note: numbers include the 2006, 25th anniversary ride based on those who indicated their intent to participate at the time this book went to print.

Ed Adams (24)	Vic Battani (24)	Rob Bellia (11)
Tom Albrecht (17)	Jim Batuk (3)	Jeff Berger (2)
Bob Alexander (1)	Greg Beck (6)	Harold Bevins (13)
Joe Baker (16)	Jim Beck (1)	Jose Bhahnik (4)
Ken Baker (20)	Butch Beckman (14)	Scott Bird (4)
Frank Balabuch (7)	David Beecherl (7)	Bill Blancke (2)
Rick Balanger (1)	Doug Beecherl (4)	Brett Bledsoe (2)
Bob Balliece (1)	Jim Beecherl (14)	Curtis Bolia (1)
Carlo Barone (2)	John Beecherl (18)	Tom Bolia (11)

Norm Bongiorno (5)

Jeff Boyd (2)

Robert Boyle (4)

Bob Bradley (24)

Bill Brandon (6)

Jeff Braum (1)

Tim Braun (1)

Gared Briggs (5)

Bob Brockett (21)

Ken Brunell (1)

Ron Bush (1)

John Cahillane (5)

David Call (6)

Lou Campbell (13)

Mike Carden (10)

Bob Carter (14)

Matt Caruso (5)

Leroy Cate (3)

Ned Cavallaro (16)

Ron Cavallaro (14)

Gene Chambers (6)

Neil Charbeneau (13)

Ray Chase (1)

Marv Claeys (10)

Doug Clancy (10)

Jarred Clion (1)

Mitch Cohoon (3)

Jack Conner (5)

Danny Cortis (8)

Dean Cueny (8)

Mike Davis (4)

Randy Decare (2)

Dick DeLange (20)

Richard DeLange (4)

Rich Demerse (3)

Bob Diehl (1)

Sue DiGiorgio (1)

Jay Dixon (7)

Rick Drinkhorn (3)

Andre Ducoffre (10)

Roger Ducoffre (7)

Fred Duemling (25)

Ken Dupell (6)

Karl Dyle (2)

Scott Eddy (4)

Greg Egan (3)

John Falkiewicz (3)

Joe Falls (2)

Abe Farrah (5)

Rich Felix (5)

Mark Fidrych (14)

Murray Finkbeiner (10)

Jeff Fiore (3)

Dennis Flynn (7)

Neil Foster (22)

Steve Foster (5)

Tom Franz (1)

Bill Freeham (5)

Frank Frisk (1)

Bob Fronrath (2)

Jim Gelios (8)

Ronald Germain (6)

Matt Giroux (16)

Randy Gmerick (3)

Jim Golds (3)

Tom Golds (10)

Don Gooley (1)

Jeff Gooley (2)

Tom Gossett (1)

Ron Grannis (2)

Al Green (22)

Kenneth Grunewald (2)

T.J. Grunewalt (8)

Rick Hacker (1)

Aldo Hafer (1)

Jeff Hamblin (1)

Carl Hart (23)

Richard Hartigan (12)

Rick Hawk (2)

Dan Hayes (6)

Mike Hazlewood (3)

Jim Heilig (9)

Roy Heisner (25)

Ken Hintz (4)

Dave Hobbs (1)

Dennis Hoffman (7)

Tim Holt (7)

Tom Imel (3)

Rick Irwin (11)

Robert Jabalee (1)

Dave Jackson (3)

Mike Jackson (2)

Tom Jackson (2)

Tom L. Jackson (1)

Bob Jantz (13)

Kerry Jantz (8)

Bill Jarvis (7)

Jim Jeffrey (5)

Wayne Jokinen (1)

Rich Jones (2)

Sam Justa (3)

Dave Kanitz (1)

Karl Kasner (13)

Hal Katterman (4)

Dennis Kavanagh (1)

George Kavanagh (3)

Tim Kavanagh (10)

Ralph Kieliszewski (15)

Larry King (25)

Roy King (21)

Joe Klinghammer (2)

Doug Koin (8)

Joe Kook (1)

Chuck Kramer (1)

Jim Kryczak (5)

Randy Kuchenmeister (3)

Gary Kukuk (22)

Kent Kukuk (2)

Steve Kukuk (5)

Tony Kulka (1)

Rick Lahousse (4)

Jim Lamb (1)

Charlie Lang (3)

Mary Lang (10)

Jim Lappan (2)

Lyn Larson (4)

Kim Leanen (11)

Clint Lee (3)

Kevin Lee (7)

Wayne Lee (6)

Dan LeGrou (8)

Paul Lemmex (1)

Tracy Leslie (3)

Donald Liposky (11)

Tom Litinas (3)

Keith Loar (3)

Hank Lorant (5)

Mike Lozon (1)

Tom Luce (2)

Mark Lufts (7)

Mike Lynch (13)

Steve Mabry (2)

Don Maes (12)

Terry Marberg (3)

Chris Malik (8)

Mike Malik (8)

Ken Maly (3)

Robert Marcereau (6)

Roy Massis (1)

Jason Mastropietro (4)

Ken Mattei (9)

Ted May (18)

Tom May (21)

Eric McAlpine (1)

Jerry McCaffrey (1)

Tom McEwen (1)

Earl McGregor (3)	John Nutt (2)	Howard Redd (22)
Allan McHenry (4)	Donald O'Dell (24)	Gene Reetz (7)
Bill McInnis (25)	Jim Olender (3)	Rick Rheeder (13)
Lee McInnis (1)	Al Oleszko (2)	Vern Rhoades (2)
Jim McKeogh (1)	Mike Osmer (6)	Ben Rizzo (4)
Mick McLatchie (2)	Gary Paja (1)	Steve Rizzo (8)
John McMullen (7)	Ed Palenkas, Sr. (1)	Jeff Robbins (4)
Pam Melby (14)	Ed Palenkas, Jr. (2)	Felix Rolando (2)
Larry Melton (2)	Joe Palmer (6)	Bob Romine (2)
Dean Meyer (6)	Rich Pardon (5)	Rita Rosek (17)
Gary Miller (1)	Tom Pardon (1)	Ron Ross (9)
Pat Modos (9)	Nick Perfili (6)	Brad Roth (6)
Monty Montmorency (1)	Steve Peters (3)	John Roth (10)
Floyd Moore (13)	Troy Petteys (2)	Dave Rouleau (2)
Jack Moore, Jr. (2)	Chuck Peyerk (10)	John Ruskus (3)
Doug Morrison (3)	Dave Pieprzak (5)	Bill Rust (1)
John Mulso (3)	Al Pilon (3)	Brian Saia (1)
Bob Myers (16)	Brad Pioch (1)	Bob Sassanella (20)
Dennis Myers (4)	Bob Pollack (5)	Wayne Schaldenbrand (17)
Vince Nasso (3)	Mike Priebe (2)	Jeff Schalm (3)
Dean Nations (6)	Mike Priemer (5)	Dan Schmuck (4)
Charlie Nemitz (11)	Jim Prince (1)	Doug Schofield (7)
Mark Nerswick (3)	Roger Pype (5)	Matt Schonsheck (4)
Leo Niedzwecki (2)	Tony Pype (24)	Ian Schonsheck (12)
Mike Nowaczk (3)	Ken Rapeer (1)	Dan Schroeder (10)
Vince Nowaczk (1)	Wayne Reams (18)	Steve Schroeder (4)

Chris Schwartz (2)	Harold Suer (3)	Gary Walser (2)
Eddy Scott (1)	Rod Szalkowski (5)	Dave Weber (22)
Todd Sharp (1)	Fred Tate ((8)	Jeff Weber (25)
Tony Silvestro (6)	Brad Teagan (9)	Tom Weber (12)
James Simpson (10)	Larry Ternes (25)	Bill Werderman (2)
Bert Sisson (10)	Frank Theut (3)	Vic Wertz (2)
Dan Slanec (3)	Rick Thierry (11)	Dave White (24)
Fred Smith (3)	Rick Thomas (4)	Tom Willhite (9)
Sam Smith (1)	Larry Tomenello (16)	Harvey Wilson (2)
Glenn Socia (5)	Colin Trainor (6)	Vince Wilson (2)
Art Sommers (4)	Neil Trainor (1)	Ed Winkowski (4)
Mike Sosnowski (4)	Don Trandal (2)	Loren Winsten (22)
Larry Spencer (1)	Howard Trombly (2)	Bryan Winsten (1)
Philip Spicer (3)	John Van Camp (7)	Mark Wysznski (3)
Jerry Spiewak (4)	Sam Ventmiglia (1)	Ryan Yakaboski (4)
Bob Spradlin (4)	Bill Verdi (5)	Dave Yonka (2)
Larry Stockmeyer (3)	Gary Vernier (4)	Jack Zendt (7)
Paul Stoltman (1)	Brett Vollen (6)	Chuck Zinner (24)
Jon Strauchman (6)	John Walker (11)	Al Zuccarro (4)
Vito Strolis (3)	Robert Waller (3)	

THE 2006, 25TH ANNIVERSARY RIDE

The 25th anniversary ride will take place January 29-February 4th, 2006. The following stops are planned:

AMERICAN LEGION — SKIDWAY LAKE

SKIDWAY MOOSE LODGE

SAND LAKE YACHT CLUB

LEOTA — RIVERSIDE BAR

LAKE CITY — TOWN PUMP

MESICK AMVETS AND MANISTEE MOOSE

MESICK SCHOOLS

FIFE LAKE

LOST CREEK SKY RANCH

CLEAR LAKE BAR

ST. HELEN AMERICAN LEGION

SILVER DOLLAR BAR — HIGGINS LAKE

SKYLINE GOLF

SWAMP BAR

KIHOOTEE'S BAR

DINGMAN'S BAR

MANCELONA SCHOOL

GREEN LANTERN — ALBA

ALBA SPORTSMEN'S CLUB

LAKES OF THE NORTH

JAKE'S PLACE — BOYNE FALLS

GARLAND RESORT

ELBOW BAR

NIGHT HAWK INN — HAWKS

CHATEAU LODGE — BLACK LAKE

PETOSKEY SNOWMOBILE CLUB

ANTRIM SNOWMOBILE CLUB

MANCELONA CLUB 131

BLACK FOREST GOLF COURSE

THE KEG BAR — WATERS

GAYLORD ARCTIC CAT DEALER

The following Warriors have indicated their intent to participate in the 25th Anniversary Ride:

Tom Albrecht	Fred Duemling	Chris Malik
Vic Battani	Rich Felix	Ken Maly
Greg Beck	Mark Fidrych	Ken Mattei
David Beecherl	Ron Germaine	Ted May
Harold Bevins	Matt Giroux	Tom May
Scott Bird	Al Green	Bill McInnis
Tom Bolia	Rick Hacker	Bob Myers
Bob Bradley	Rick Hawk	Mike Nowaczyk
Bob Brockett	Mike Hazlewood	Digger O'Dell
John Cahillane	Roy Heisner	Joe Palmer
David Call	Sam Justa	Steve Peters
Lou Campbell	Karl Kasner	David Pieprzak
Mike Carden	Tim Kavanagh	Tony Pype
Rob Carter	Larry King	Wayne Reams
Ned Cavallaro	Roy King	Howard Redd
Ron Cavallaro	Doug Koin	Gene Reetz
Doug Clancy	Randy Kuchenmeister	Rick Rheeder
Jarred Cloin	Gary Kukuk	Vern Rhoades
Mike Davis	Steve Kukuk	Felix Rolanda
Dick DeLange	Kim Laenen	Bob Romine
Richard DeLange	Charles Lang	John Ruskus
Sue DiGiorgio	Kevin Lee	Bob Sassanella
Jay Dixon	Mike Lynch	Wayne Schaldenbrand

Matt Schonsheck	Rick Thomas	Jeff Weber
Bert Sisson	Larry Tomenello	Tom Weber
Larry Stockmeyer	Gary Vernier	Dave White
Fred Tate	Brett Vollen	Winnie Winsten
Larry Ternes	John Walker	Mark Wyszynski
Frank Theut	Gary Walser	Ryan Yakaboski
Richard Thierry	Dave Weber	Chuck Zinner

CHAPTER 15

Special Olympics Michigan Honors

AWARDS

Ken Baker was the 1998 recipient of the President's Award* for his work with the Water Warriors, a sister organization that conducts an endurance water ride from Mackinaw City to Harsens Island near St. Clair Shores. Ken was an early rider and leader of the Wertz Warriors organization.

Fred Duemling was a recipient of the 2001 President's Award* for his work on the Wertz Warriors.

President's Award now called the Board Chair Award.

MEMBERS OF THE SPECIAL OLYMPICS MICHIGAN BOARD OF DIRECTORS

Vic Battani served for six years on the board of directors of Special Olympics Michigan and served a year as president of the board. In 2003, Dave Weber was elected to the board for a three-year term.

CHAPTER 16

The Rides Go On

Even though we have come to the end of this commemorative book, celebrating 25 years of rides and giving to Special Olympics athletes, the rides will continue. But let us pause and look back a bit one last time.

Who are these men? Tim Kavanagh states it well, "The Warriors come from all walks of life: doctors, lawyers, laborers, mechanics, computer programmers — and yes, even former baseball stars. Some are rich and some not-so-rich. But despite all our differences, I think we all have one thing in common; we simply want to help those less fortunate than we are and the Special Olympics Michigan happened to be an organization that fit the bill."

Tony Pype summarizes the feelings of all Warriors when he says, "In my 24 years I have met hundreds of new friends, had millions of laughs. I have seen smiles and heard the laughter of thousands of athletes. It really doesn't get old, helping others. I feel I could never repay what I have gotten out of my involvement with Wertz Warriors and Special Olympics Michigan."

Larry Ternes speaks for most Warriors in conclusion, "When I first became involved back in 1982, I never realized we would come so far ... through the years my life has been touched by so many people, not just within our organization but other people who have helped us with our fund-raisers, these people alone make a person realize that there still is hope for mankind, there is still kindness in people and there are those who still believe in his fellow man. This realization is a common thread that has held us together for so many years and it has become an inner part of our own families. I see it in my sons ... they were so young when I first was a Warrior but through the years they have shared with me a part of life that can only be experienced through acts of kindness and the abilities of the Special Olympians to portray their own gratitude for being a unique part of their world ... the role of a Warrior. In my sons' eyes ... I have grown, not with age but with acts of kindness, a sense of well-being and the willingness to do what is right, not just for yourself but for the person standing next to you. These rights of passage will never be conveyed in a classroom, nor will they be illustrated in a book ... but they will be taught by a person who is less fortunate but yet so blessed by the simple truths of life ... honesty, innocence and a sense of accomplishment no matter how insignificant. As Warriors, these are our rewards ... and I hope and pray every one of us past or present has realized this ... for we will never be the same."

WERTZ WARRIORS AUTOGRAPHS

2015

Bob Myers

MIKE #10

R. BROCKET

Jay Dixon

Howard Redd

Diggin Odell

Toby

16

Wayne Reams

Boomer

#17

#20

#59

VERN Rhoades